Irina Odoevtseva
Poet, Novelist, Memoirist

Irina Odoevtseva

POET, NOVELIST, MEMOIRIST

A Literary Portrait

by Ella Bobrow

*Nasledie Publishing
at the Gorky Institute of World Literature
of the Russian Academy of Science
Published Ella Bobrow's book in Russian in 1995*

Mosaic Press
Oakville, ON. - Buffalo, N.Y.

Canadian Cataloguing in Publication Data

Bobrow, Ella, 1911 -
    Irina Odoevtseva, poetess, novelist, memoirist : a literary portrait

Includes poetry by Irina Odoevtseva.
ISBN 0-88962-600-6

1. Odoevtseva, Irina Vladimirovna, 1901-   -Biography.
I. Odoevtseva, Irina Vladimirovna, 1901-   .II. Title.

PG3476.I857Z53   1996   891.7'8   C95-933364-9

No part of this book may be reproduced or transmitted in any form, by any means, electronic or mechanical, including photocopying and recording information storage and retrieval systems, without permission in writing from the publisher, except by a reviewer who may quote brief passages in a review.

Published by MOSAIC PRESS, P.O. Box 1032, Oakville, Ontario, L6J 5E9, Canada. Offices and warehouse at 1252 Speers Road, Units #1&2, Oakville, Ontario, L6L 5N9, Canada and Mosaic Press, 85 River Rock Drive, Suite 202, Buffalo, N.Y., 14207, USA.

Mosaic Press acknowledges the assistance of the Canada Council, the Ontario Arts Council and the Dept. of Canadian Heritage, Government of Canada, for their support of our publishing programme.

Copyright © Ella Bobrow, 1996

Cover and book design by Susan Parker
Printed and bound in Canada
ISBN   0-88962-600-6

In Canada:
MOSAIC PRESS, 1252 Speers Road, Units #1&2, Oakville, Ontario, L6L 5N9, Canada. P.O. Box 1032, Oakville, Ontario, L6J 5E9
In the United States:
MOSAIC PRESS, 85 River Rock Drive, Suite 202, Buffalo, N.Y., 14207
In the UK and Western Europe:
DRAKE INTERNATIONAL SERVICES, Market House, Market Place, Deddington, Oxford. OX15 OSF

I lovingly dedicate this work to Leon Zuckert, for many years my husband, friend and collaborator.

Acknowledgement

I would like to express my deepest
appreciation and gratitude to
my family and all my friends
whose encouragement and support
made this publication possible.

Contents

Author's Note	ix
Foreword: Christopher Barnes	xiii
Biographical Note	xvi

POETRY

Odoevtseva's Poetry	1
Selected Poems	11
The Ballads	13
Irina Odoevtseva's Short Prose	30

NOVELS

The Angel of Death ("Angel Smerti")	34
Isolde ("Isolda")	43
The Mirror ("Zerkalo")	64
One Year In A Life ("God Zhizni")	78
Abandon Hope Forever ("Ostav' Nadezhdu Navsegda")	91

MEMOIRS

On The Banks of The Neva (" Na Beregakh Nevy")	105
Alexander Blok	108
Osip Mandelstam	109
Nikolai Gumilyov	110
Andrei Bely	117

Mikhail Kuzmin	121
Fyodor Sologub	123
On The Banks of The Seine ("Na Beregakh Seny")	126
Marina Tsvetaeva	129
Konstantin Balmont	131
Igor Severyanin	132
Sergei Esenin	133
Boris Poplavsky	133
Nadezhda Teffi	134
Georgi Adamovich	136
Ivan Bunin	139
Boris Zaitsev	143
The Merezhkovskys	144
Georgi Ivanov	148
Yuri Terapiano	152
Yakov Gorbov	153
Yuri Annenkov	154
Sergei Sharshun	155
Bibliography	157
Russian	
In Translation	
References	158

Author's Note

"Ballads are dedicated and monuments erected to people only after their death..." -- This was Irina Odoevtseva's jocular answer to poet Nikolai Gumilyov's suggestion that she write a ballad about his life and works. Their exchange took place at Christmas time in 1920. At that time she could not have known that the following spring he would be arrested and shot and that she would be writing about him three years later, in Paris.

How different would the literary portraits of Odoevtseva's contemporaries have been had she created them while they were still alive?

The late Russian émigré writer Yuri Ivask once expressed regret that monographs are rarely written about living authors, for they could be the first, and perhaps the most reliable, source of information about their own lives and works. Is this implied reproach to scholars and researchers justified? One recalls Gumilyov's own complaint about portrait artists who always concealed the squint which he referred to as God's mark; or Winston Churchill's disgust with his sculptured image, widely considered a "masterpiece" but which he called a "monster".

It was after reading Odoevtseva's memoirs *On the Banks of the Neva* ("Na beregakh Nevy") that I first thought of writing a monograph about her. However, knowing the limitations as well as the advantages this subject would impose, I quickly rejected the idea of a traditional, scholarly, documented monograph. Instead I decided on a poetical improvisation, completely free of canons and with research concentrating mainly on Odoevtseva's own works, on the themes of her poetry, the characters of her novels, and especially on her own memoirs. I wanted to create her literary portrait. I even began writing this work in verse, planning a new form of semi-historical poem with a free choice of rhythmic pattern, reflecting the pulse of her time and the change of events.

"As a child she had dreamt of becoming a poet and only a poet, not a glorious swan on the stage, not a star of the screen. And she knew that her wish would come true when she met a great poet by the river Neva in one thousand nine hundred eighteen..."

At that time I was also invited to lecture about another émigré poet Dmitri Klenovsky, whose work I greatly admire. Favourable press reviews of this (*Novy Zhurnal,* of New York published two such lectures of mine) brought further invitations to Los Angeles, Washington, Montreal and Toronto -- cities where I subsequently appeared with a lecture about Irina Odoevtseva and "The image of Russia in the works of her poets". These events eventually led me to reject the idea of semi-historical poetic improvisation about Odoevtseva and persuaded me instead to plan a prose monograph. By extensively studying her works -- poetry, ballads, novels and especially her memoirs -- I hoped to create a portrait of Odoevtseva that would avoid distortion as well as excessive glorification.

Most of Odoevtseva's books were published in the West in Russian, only a few in English, German, French and Spanish many years ago. They are no longer accessible to readers. Therefore, instead of following the usual convention and citing endless page numbers, I found it more logical to support my judgements with ample quotations from the original. Thus, Odoevtseva's literary portrait is, to a certain degree, a self-portrait.

As a prime source of information, I did not find Odoevtseva very helpful, since she disliked talking about herself. During our meetings in Paris she preferred talking about others. The two of us worked for many hours and days on restoring the lost manuscript of the second volume of her memoirs, *On the Bank of the Seine*. During rare moments of conversation about her own past, she inevitably changed the subject and reminisced instead about her contemporaries. Her comments were always fascinating but rarely answered my questions. Nevertheless, I am happy to be able to share with readers some details about the birth of her novels and her memoirs. Knowing how much she always appreciated my work on this book, I used to send her the first draft of each chapter from Toronto, or from Spain, where I continued writing during our winter vacations.

One might wonder whether Odoevtseva acted as a "censor" of my writings about her and of my interpretations of her works. In fact she probably sensed the sincerity of my conclusions, based on thoughtful research and study of her heroes, and she was therefore too kind to be critical of my work. Yet I do recall a difference of opinion concerning the youthful heroine of her novel *Isolde*. Odoevtseva found my judgment of Isolde's involvement in the terrible crime somewhat too harsh. But on my side was the actual book, and rereading my quotations from it confirmed me in my conclusions. She told me on several occasions that her late husband Georgi Ivanov would have been very pleased with my work. After returning from Paris to Russia in April of 1987, she repeatedly expressed a desire to see my book published there.

Both volumes of her memoirs were published in Moscow in 1988 and 1989 (over a million copies were sold). But most of her poetry, her ballads, short stories and novels are still not available to the broad circle of Russian readers. The publication in the periodical press of excerpts from this work and the subsequent appearance of the Russian original of the book about Odoevtseva in today's Russia will no doubt raise readers' demand for her out-of-print works and lead to their publication in the very near future.

It may take years before all Odoevtseva's works are available to readers in Russia. But there is new hope that the present book about her will be published in the very near future, and this will bring Irina Odoevtseva closer to all those who are eager to know more about her works that still remain out of print.

Ella Bobrow.

Foreword

Publication of this, the first monograph on Irina Odoevtseva, is a long overdue event. Ella Bobrow, the poetess' long-standing friend and admirer, completed her book more than a decade ago. Only the vicissitudes of Soviet and Russian émigré literary politics forestalled the book's immediate and deserved appearance in the early 1980's. (The Albatross Publishers in Paris made a last minute politically motivated decision not to bring out the book after Odoevtseva had returned to Russia, though the manuscript was already typeset). Now it appears in both Russian and English.

In the light of history, though, more significant are the decades of Odoevtseva's enforced exile in France, which almost to the end of her life prevented recognition in her native country as one of the prominent figures of St. Petersburg and Russian émigré literature. The standing that Irina Odoevtseva truly deserves has hitherto been apparent mainly to readers and scholars familiar with her poems, fiction and memoirs. For those still in doubt or ignorance, however, Ella Bobrow's book will serve as a broad introduction to one of Russia's major woman writers.

Delays and silence notwithstanding, Odoevtseva is fortunate in having Ella Bobrow as her first biographer and monographer. A kindly fate guided Bobrow towards her chosen subject, and we as readers share this good fortune. The empathy between author and subject is rooted in several years of meetings, correspondence, collaboration and evident mutual admiration that initially stemmed from Odoevtseva's several visits to Canada and America. The story of their relationship is to a certain degree presented in the pages that follow. Their communion was also celebrated in a moving exchange of poetic messages and dedications between Bobrow and Odoevtseva, which strike more forcefully in the original Russian. One such poem, of January 1969, records Bobrow's own joy that Odoevtseva in her happiness was "not scattered long ago like star dust over the earth", but was "able to awake on the bank of your native Neva our city of geniuses that slept for half a century..." The reference here was to Odoevtseva's memoirs that evoked such vivid memories of old Petersburg and the literary pleiade to which she belongs. But in part, too, the image could be extended to Bobrow's own literary-biographical study in the present book.

    The fates and personalities of both author and subject in the pages that follow have much in common. Aside from the "coincidence" of their being women of letters, prominent poets and prose authors, there is in both of them a shared sense of loss and nostalgia. They possess a compensating heightened ability to treasure happy moments or experiences with a poignancy that only those familiar with prolonged emigration and exile can fully appreciate. The experiences of Odoevtseva recorded in verse, projected and fleshed out in prose fiction, or set down in more direct memoir form, are thus intensified and refracted through the double prism of her own and her biographer's personality.

    The result is something that differs from a conventional biography or standardized academic monograph. It is closer to that canon-free "poetic improvisation" on the theme of Odoevtseva's life and work of which Bobrow herself writes in her Author's Note. Included are English-language poetic recreations of her ballads, numerous other poetic extracts, and aptly evocative quotations from Odoevtseva's novels.

    At the same time, Ella Bobrow has not ignored the expectations of those who come to this book in search of concrete information about Odoevtseva. Because many of her writings (particularly her prose) are at the moment inaccessible, we urgently need (and find in this book) a fundamental introduction to and record of these works that will convey a sense of plots, settings, characters, with stylistic subtlety. Odoevtseva's lyrical prose returns us to a now bygone age and a vanished lifestyle on the fringe of the Russian émigré world -- contemporary to, but totally lacking in the tantalizing hallucinatory qualities of Nabokov's tales set in the Russian emigration.

Ella Bobrow also skillfully reveals the essence of Odoevtseva's memoiristic writings *On the Banks of the Neva* and *On the Banks of the Seine* without retelling the narrative, yet preserving the main value of these reminiscences. From the innumerable scattered strands of recollection running through Odoevtseva's two books Bobrow has used excerpts and summary to weave a coherent series of vignettes which stand in their own right. These also present an alluring portrait gallery as well as (for the researcher) a handy reference manual of literary personalities with whom Odoevtseva lived and communed for several decades. Bobrow's book should indeed appeal in equal measure to specialists and students, as well as to general readers interested in modern Russian literature. To record and applaud its appearance is both a privilege and a pleasure.

Christopher Barnes

University of Toronto,
June 1994.

Biographical Note
Irina Odoevtseva

Irina Odoevtseva tells us in her memoirs that from her early youth she had always wanted to become a poet and only a poet. But neither she nor her illustrious teacher, the poet Nikolai Gumilyov, knew in the early twenties that, besides poems and ballads, she would gain fame with her novels, her short stories, and especially her memoirs in which she revived the triumph and tragedy of many of her contemporaries, the poets and writers of Russian literature's "Silver Age". Although she mastered four major languages in childhood, especially French, she wrote all her life in Russian only, and thus she remained part of Russian émigré literature.

The course of Irina Odoevtseva's life was unusual. In her youth, she earned fame in post-revolutionary Petrograd (the former and future St. Petersburg) as a poet and as the author-inventor of the contemporary ballad. She left for the West in the early twenties, following her husband, the poet Georgi Ivanov.

Although a repetition of the pronoun *I* in memoirs is natural, Irina Odoevtseva's recollections do not give much biographical information. And this is not surprising. In the short foreword to the first volume she states: "I am writing not *about* myself, and not *for* myself, but about all those whom I was fortunate to know on the banks of the Neva." Yet we see Odoevtseva's reflection on the pages of her novels and in the lines of her poems; we hear her voice in conversations with her contemporaries vividly recounted in her memoirs; we silently listen with her to the monologues of Andrei Bely, Gumilyov, Ivan Bunin and others who appreciated her gift of listening; and between the lines of her writings we find an adolescent, hungry for love and attention, a young girl in love with poetry, and a startlingly beautiful woman who loves life despite all its setbacks and tragedies. Yet these grains of information are scattered on the hundreds of pages of her book and they leave readers still searching for the kind of detail that would create a picture of the author. I will try here to add something to this image.

In the concise Soviet Literary Encyclopedia, Odoevtseva's name is mentioned in volumes two, five and eight, though the information given is not always correct and complete: "Odoevtseva Irina Vladimirovna (pseudonym; real name Irina Gustavovna Geinike, born 1901, Riga) -- a Russian poetess, active member of the Poets' Guild ("Tsekh Poetov")[1]-- Acmeists..." [2]

In fact Odoevtseva's correct birthdate was July 24, 1895. The Soviet Literary Encyclopedia gives titles and publication dates of her novels and poetry collections, yet not a word is said about her 37-year-long marriage to the Russian émigré poet Georgi Ivanov. As the daughter of an attorney, her childhood was never marred by poverty. She learnt to speak German, English, and French fluently, and to read European classical literature in the original.

Even after the revolution her parents lived in the large apartment of an old aristocratic house with a study-library complete with a fireplace -- a luxury not many people could afford at that time. Although there were rarely logs for the fire, and although the family had just as little to eat as other Soviet

---

[1] "Poets' Guild" -- Tsekh poetov -- a literary organization (1911 - 1914) in St. Petersburg -- revived in 1921 - 1923.

[2] Acmeists -- represented by Gumilyov, Akhmatova, Mandelstam, Kuzmin and others -- proclaimed the return in poetry to precise definition of things of nature and everyday life.

citizens, the young Irina maintained a bourgeois appearance and would never leave the house without a hat and gloves.

Her employment record book was used for the first time when she enrolled in November 1918 in the poetry course at the *Living Word* Institute ("Zhivoye Slovo"). This date and event open her memoirs, *On the Banks of the Neva* ("Na beregakh Nevy"). In the entire volume her family is hardly mentioned; even the death of her mother is passed over lightly. It is as if life for her began right there, in St. Petersburg, the city she would forever call her own, the city where her wish to become a poet came true despite moments of uncertainty and doubt, expressed in the following lines dated 1918:

> I won't be known around the globe
> Nor will be ever crowned by fame;
> To this I have just as much claim,
> As I have to a bishop's robe.
>
> My teacher or the wicked press
> Won't choose me for a talent show.
> I'm just a little poetess
> With an enormous bow.

Forty years later, she recalls this time in another poem:

> Yes, no question, my life's beginning
> Promised everything, laughing and singing
> In St. Petersburg on the Neva.
> Fate fulfilled many a childhood dream,
> Granting me what I deemed most dear
> Without miserly haggling -- here!
>
> Days were sunlit, the nights were starry,
> Past and future were ousted by "now".
> Flying by, just in passing, glory
> Touched my still adolescent brow.

Odoevtseva still remembered that in spite of the terror that raged around her during those years, in spite of feeling cold and hungry at home most of the time, for her life was starting as an adventure into new worlds that all the books she had read had never revealed. Gumilyov... It was not easy to study with him. He had no mercy on his students. According to his theory, one cannot and should not write poems without having studied poetry. He would say: "Only when you know all the rules, can you, as Calderon taught, lock them away in a drawer and throw the key into the sea... I can't breathe talent into your mind, yet what you now call inspiration is just ignorance and illiteracy."

When the "Literary Studio" was established in 1919, Irina Odoevtseva was the only one from the class of the *Living Word* Institute whom Gumilyov "upgraded" as his student. He gave her books from his own library to widen her knowledge of literature, history, and philosophy. He made her read Nietzsche, Schopenhauer and, of course, foreign poetry. He would speak proudly of her progress, introducing her everywhere as "my pupil Irina Odoevtseva".

It was Nikolai Gumilyov through whom she soon became part of the circle of poets and writers. In the first volume of her memoirs, his name appears almost on every page. To her, he personified poetry. He taught her to become a poet, not a follower but a poet with her own voice. Even for Georgi Ivanov, who later became her husband, she has only a few sentences. Here is how she describes their first meeting: "I silently shook hands with him. For the first time. No, without any premonition."

Always reluctant to speak about her private life, she avoids mentioning any events in her life outside literature. Thus Georgi Ivanov and her second husband Yakov Gorbov appear in her memoirs only because the first was a poet and the second a writer.

In 1921 she accompanied her husband to Berlin; they later moved to France. Her father had earlier left Russia for Riga. After his death, she inherited a large house and was thus able to buy one in Biarritz, which allowed her and her husband to live comfortably until the Second World War, when all her property was destroyed by bombs.

In France, though surrounded by writers and poets, Odoevtseva could not find the fervent interest in poetry she had known during the years in St. Petersburg. She soon turned to prose. Her first published short story *A Shooting Star* ("Paduchaya zvezda"), was an immediate success.

In 1927 her first novel *Angel of Death* ("Angel smerti") brought her even more praise from readers and reviewers. During the period from 1927 to 1957 four more of her novels were published.

In 1958 her husband died in Hyeres, Southern France. She was admitted to a residence for writers and poets in Gagny near Paris. There she wrote her memoirs.

In 1967 Victor Kamkin, Inc. in Washington published *On the Banks of the Neva*. The great success of this first volume brought Odoevztseva invitations from the United States and Canada. She appeared at many universities and was interviewed on several radio programs.

In 1978 she married Yakov Gorbov, a writer, who had earned fame in France for his novels in French, a language he had mastered since his childhood. He was also co-editor of the Russian periodical *La Renaissance* ("Vozrozhdenie"). They lived together in Paris until his death in 1981.

In 1983 *La Press* in Paris published the second volume of Odoevtseva's memoirs *On the Banks of the Seine* ("Na beregakh Seny"). She was delighted by its success and full of hope for more encounters with readers, especially those in the United States and Canada. *On the Banks of the Seine* was Odoevtseva's last literary success in the West.

Unfortunately, due to an injured hip, she found herself ill and in no position to travel. Yet neither prolonged hospitalization nor repeated operations on the hip broke her courage and will to live. When I visited her in a Paris hospital on March 22, 1986, on my way back from Spain, she was still full of hope that

she would regain the ability to walk and resume work on her next book.
Alas, back home in a wheel chair she was faced with the impossibility of living alone as an invalid. All her friends' attempts to find tenants who would be willing to share the spacious four-room apartment in exchange for helping her failed. Friends would come and visit but had to return to their families. This very difficult time coincided with the rehabilitation of several émigré writers and poets in Russia. Odoevtseva also heard of relatives on her mother's side who now contacted her after 60 years of silence. The never extinguished hope for a wide circle of Russian readers finally seemed within reach. All this made her contemplate and finally accept an invitation from the Soviet government to return to Leningrad, where she was promised not only a similar apartment but also housekeeping and medical care, a literary secretary and new publications of all her works, as well as her husband's. On April 11, 1987 she boarded a plane in Paris, accompanied by a Soviet medical doctor, and settled in the city of her youth.

She was later visited in Russia by many friends and admirers from Europe, the USA and Canada. They all confirmed that she was in a happy mood and lacked nothing in her everyday life. She felt overwhelmed by attention from radio and television. Many of her poems and excerpts from her prose have since been republished in Russia by the periodical press, and both volumes of her memoirs *On the Banks of the Neva* and *On the Banks of the Seine* are now available to Russian readers in new editions (1988 -- 1989).

She was especially thrilled and overjoyed by the flood of enthusiastic readers' letters. On October 31, 1988, she wrote to me, rephrasing her own verses: ''Now life here is for me a true delight!'' This euphoria was reaffirmed by further letters with enclosed programs from concerts and poetry readings in Moscow and Peredelkino.

In August of 1989 my daughter and I visited her at a writers' retreat in Komarovo. Despite the immense success of her republished memoirs, which sold millions of copies, her mood at that time was somewhat subdued. Aside from health problems, she was saddened that republication of her poetry and novels was delayed by lack of paper and general economic difficulties in the country. Another cause for sadness was the constant change of helpers, especially literary secretaries.

One can understand that in her situation it was not easy to select nobly motivated people among the many instant friends who surrounded her -- a famous, relatively wealthy, but physically helpless writer. It is still harder to judge from afar the true motives of her new friends. Yet, knowing some aspects of their activities, I would like to mention a few of them.

Anna Kolonitsky and Alexander Sabov were supportive in Paris when Odoevtseva had to make the fateful decision to return to Russia. Kolonitsky later energetically looked after Odoevtseva's daily needs and managed her financial affairs, including royalties from the sale of books. Sabov and his wife Irina devoted much of their time to preparing Odoevtseva's memoirs for republishing, and even undertook the editing of her husband Yakov Gorbov's letters to his first wife, letters which turned out to be an original chronicle of Russian émigré life and literature. Zoya N. Kuznetsova was a constant unofficial help from the very beginning and kept me informed about Odoevtseva's life when her secretary failed to do so.

Especially valuable to Odoevtseva as a writer was the help and co-operation of Honoured Actress of the Russian Federation Tamara Voronina, her first literary secretary. She also applied some alternative methods of treating her hip and leg; Odoevtseva was even able to stand up and make a few steps. Unfortunately, the treatment had to be interrupted when she moved back from Moscow to Leningrad.

The innumerable literary evenings and concert-readings from her works brought much joy to the author, the performer, and to the public. But Odoevtseva's hope to write again did not materialize. She could no longer concentrate on dictating, since her health was constantly deteriorating.

On October 14, 1990, at the age of 95, she passed away in her apartment in St. Petersburg. She was buried in the

Volkovskoye cemetery. The quiet funeral was arranged by the Writers' Union. She died with the hope that sooner or later all her works would be republished and read by the Russian readers who had greeted her return with such enthusiasm and had showered her with letters full of well deserved love and gratitude. After all, despite her mastery of several European languages and the decades spent in a foreign literary climate, Odoevtseva wrote only in Russian. She always thought of the Russian readers who in her youth had crowned her with a "short, fleeting fame", always hoping to be heard by them again some day. And they joyously accepted her gift to them and to Russian literature.

* * *

Odoevtseva's Poetry

I know it would be fruitless to define and describe the magic of Odoevtseva's poetry. I therefore invite you to listen to the ever-changing, capricious voice of her muse, in order to fill in the missing features of her literary portrait: her outlook on life, youth and age; on love and beauty, good and evil, and on death -- on everything that inevitably touches the poet's mind and heart and is reflected in her poetry.

The poet Nikolai Gumilyov, her teacher and mentor, maintained that even as a beginner she sang with her own voice, never imitating other poets, despite her admiration for them -- especially for Anna Akhmatova.

The range of themes in her poetry is very wide, and she usually touches on several in any one poem. Her contradictory and apparently unconnected thoughts race and chase and overtake one another. This seeming inconsistency appears even in her early poems. A 1924 piece begins with an ordinary line: "I'm writing Christmas greetings to my family across the ocean..." At first sight, there is nothing original in this theme. But the poet's thoughts are already outside the window, where there is "frosty air and starry ringing..." where to encounter a poetic adventure "the perturbed soul flies over heavenly fragile petals,/ Scaring the moonlit little frogs,/ The maiden-friends join hurrying..." Thus the poet interrupts the task of writing greeting cards to describe a dream and her awakening at the same desk, crowded with books.

In a much more serious, yet just as inconsistent vein, Odoevtseva uses the writer Remizov's words: "Chelovek cheloveku brevno". (One man is a block [of wood] to another.) And in confirmation of his thought, she begins with a line full of weltschmerz: "Indifference is death to the lonely and suffering ones." Yet quickly she moves to a lighter tone: "...to vagabonds, fools and poets/ Who are known for their twisted brain/ Loneliness is nonsense and folly. / They mock at compassion and need no cheering..." Odoevtseva then turns to describe the night after a day of hard labour: "It is so dark you can't see a thing [zgi] in front of your nose..." Then, suddenly, she explodes angrily and passionately in a stanza calling upon an imaginary "Zga" -- a power that would "light up the dark, sparkling and ringing in its flight, rise sky-high with lightning speed and crash down in flames onto the house, like a firespewing, smoke-emitting column; turn into black horror, scarlet shame to become the most just conviction..." Then just as suddenly and unexpectedly, she assumes a calmly philosophical tone, concluding: "Thus once perished Sodom/ And Gomorra."

In some of Odoevtseva's early poems logic and classical form still prevailed, however. There were no sudden changes of tone and mood, no capricious rhythms or broken lines in poems on the death of Gumilyov and on "True Love". At that time, perhaps, she dared not follow Calderon's advice to lock all acquired rules in a drawer and throw the key into the sea. This is not to say that she ever rejected all rules and joined the avantgarde. She never arbitrarily broke lines, discarding punctuation marks, capital letters, etc., out of fear of appearing old-fashioned. Most of her poems of the fifties, and even of the 1970s, are fairly traditional in form. Despite her "question, / More venomous than vitriol/ Could one still write poems/ Seriously?.." -- her poems of those years are marked by a consistent mood. One such poem is full of self-accusation and grief: "I cannot forgive myself/ Although I have forgiven all the others..." Odoevtseva writes in this key very rarely. She more often has-

tens to assure the reader that "Life is still the most delightful/ Of all enjoyable affairs."
Love of life is reflected in both her early and her mature poetry. "It's joy to have life as a friend, /Our bondage could never be broken." She wrote these lines in post-revolutionary Petersburg, despite the often unheated rooms and scarcity of food. No blows of fate could break her friendship with life. And even in the 1980s, the leitmotif of her poetry remained: "In light of day, in dreams of night, / Life to me is sheer delight."
Odoevtseva's passionate love of life arouses no fear of death: it only deepens her desire to prolong the joy of living. Thus she asks the little goldfish: "Let me live to a hundred years / And then add a few more of eternity." She herself is at times amazed at her ability to enjoy life. "Though it seems nothing could be sadder, / bleaker or more hopeless than my fate, / Joyously still beats my heart..."
However, her optimistic, life-asserting poems are at times clouded by the inevitable nostalgia of an émigré poet. Yet she expresses this only poetically and makes no political statements, protests, or accusations. She does not refer to her "motherland," but instead describes how "The wind, ringing of space, returns to Kreshchensky parade, / To my dear Petrograd..."
It is impossible to list all the poems that express Odoevtseva's love for Russia. Yet, as a "barefooted pilgrim", she harbours no illusions about returning there in her lifetime. Therefore: "I firmly believe that in paradise / I shall find my land anew / That only in Heaven shall I be at home..."
The word "proshloye" (the past) often finds its way into her poems. Yet she does not idealize the past and does not dwell on memories. Genuine sadness sounds in lines such as these: "It is not true, never true / That the past is dear to me: / It is like a grave, greedily open / And I'm horrified to look into it..."
Although fate often gave her reason to say "how little warmth one finds on Earth, / How often one finds cold and evil," an all-forgiving affinity with the world is much more characteristic of her poetry.

"Every living creature, every object makes me perceive a sense of brotherhood and sisterhood and makes me aware day and night of my indissoluble kinship with the world." On rereading, her poems with their many striking images no longer sound merely personal. We read in them of anguish "sprinkled with caustic salt of grief" and of "the double-bottom of despair"; and finally, the expectation of a miracle: "That from your grave you'd suddenly appear / And come toward me, alive and full of cheer." The emotions expressed sound so familiar to us that we recognize them as our own. The poet seems to know it and addresses us directly:

> The heart of a stranger (yours, my reader?
> Yours, dreamer?
> Yours, passerby?)
> Beats within me as my own.

Odoevtseva's intimate relationship with humanity's "brotherhood-sisterhood" finds especially distinct expression in the theme of loneliness. Though she often claimed that human contacts gave her pleasure, there is an unmistakable authenticity in her confession:

> I'm terrified when I'm alone,
> And even more so when with others
> In a noisy merry-go-round:
> So terrified I cannot bear it.

Yet elsewhere, as if aware that her readers identify with her, she wrote: "Loneliness and weariness / Make me feel a wave of / Tender, warm compassion / For myself and other beings in the world."

In Odoevtseva's youth this closeness to the world was perhaps subconscious, though in her very early poems we find lines such as: "God bless all disconsolate ones!" Much later, wise from experience and observation, she exclaims: "Which of all tortures could compare / With loneliness?" And she stretches out her hand, trying to reach "one with a common fate: My faraway friend and brother on this planet with me. / Are you not glad that we have met ?.." Still on this theme, the poet's thoughts turn to man's aspiration to reach other planets as a way of relieving the painful "loneliness of a star". She listens to the voices of cosmonauts and shares their experience in space. Odoevtseva's poetical meditations are, however, unlike the *Gedankenlyrik* of other poets. She seems to touch the theme of loneliness in passing, yet reaches the highest point of concentration in the lines: "My loneliness. Your loneliness. Ours. Yours. Their loneliness."

Despite melancholy, sad, or even tragic notes, her poetry never becomes downcast or dismal. The thought that "Life has passed..." is followed by another: "But youth lingers on... I have never been as happy as I am now." Unable, maybe, to hide her grief, she repeats like an incantation: "I'm happy, I'm happy, I'm happy..." as a shield to protect herself from the pity or compassion that could insult her pride.

Odoevtseva dispels all thoughts about the inevitable end: "No, wise old age, neither in my life, nor in my poems -- I do not go your way until my death." Yet in a group of "Poems written during an illness" ("Stikhi, napisannye vo vremya bolezni") not once is the word "death" mentioned. And although in a semi-delirious state, she once pleads: "Do not let me die!" we cannot find in Odoevtseva's poetry any lines expressing fear of death.

For Odoevtseva, to die means to live on: "Following the angels, on transparent glass stairs / We shall rise to paradise..." We find her first description of the beyond in a poem about Gumilyov's death by firing squad in 1921:
"There is a cool breeze in blue paradise, / And the air is fresh and pure, / And the trees rustle above, / Like the trees of the Summer Garden." Perhaps ever since that time Odoevtseva's poetry was illuminated by a belief that one should not cry, that there is a new life (life again!), no longer in a rented room in Paris, but in paradise, where there is light and peace forever and ever.

Yet her belief in paradise does not prevent Odoevtseva from enjoying life on earth: "Now, at my sunset golden hours, /

When the play is almost finished / When clouds are covering the skies... / I'm happier now than ever before."
Readers may wonder what it was that helped Odoevtseva to survive and forget the many blows of fate? What healed the wounds inflicted by life? What made her live on, loving life and enjoying every moment of existence?
When we analyze the female characters of her novels, we often find points of similarity with the author. What dominates the destiny of her heroines is love and its absorbing power. It is love that motivates their actions; love is the sole *raison d'être* for life and happiness; and love, if lost, is the source of their ultimate and unconquerable boundless grief and despair.
How then is love reflected in Odoevtseva's poetry? Here are some lines from a very early poem of 1921: "The moon sends me the sweet breeze of a promise / The promise of a great true-hearted love. / But sadness does not dare desire happiness / May God bless all the sad and mournful ones!" One year later, already a married woman, Odoevtseva dedicated to her husband some humorous lines asking "Love... What is its definition?.. / On the water's surface I write confessions of love / Build blue enchanted castles in the air..." Much later, Odoevtseva recalled an unforgettable encounter in St. Petersburg's Summer Gardens, when she arrived two hours late: "He only raised his left eye-brow / And looked at me... Yet / Not a single word of reproach. / Then I said to myself: This is love."
In Odoevtseva's sparkling poetry there are many poems about love. Often it is only implied, as if the author shares her thoughts with the reader in strict confidence. We shall discuss one such poem below, without trying to find out what inspired it or under what circumstances it was written. The poem is dated 1922. Countless songs and poems about love have been created ever since the concept came into being. Examples abound especially in Russian lyric verse and music. Yet this particular poem is not about the all-absorbing, at times destructive, power of passion. It deals instead with a love that is capable of sacrifice for the sake of others and in the name of higher values. Although

my translation may not reveal its perfection of form or the
originality of its metaphor, here is the whole poem in English:

> Then he said: "Farewell, my dear.
> From now on
> I may never meet you here again."
> Down the alley I walked on. Where was I?
> In the Summer Garden or in Hell?
>
> Quiet. Empty. Gates are locked. No exit.
> Now, what is the sense of going home?
> Something white moves on along dark alleys,
> blindly stumbling. I was not alone.
>
> Now it stood right next to me: a statue,
> softly sparkling in the full moon's light.
> Then it spoke, its voice was slightly muffled,
> and it looked at me with eyes all white.
>
> "If you wish, we could, perhaps, change places,
> since a marble heart would never ache.
> You would be of marble, I'd be living.
> Come up here and take my bow and shield."
>
> "Very well," I answered, "I am ready.
> Have my shoes, my coat, and all that's mine."
> Taking them, the statue kissed me lightly,
> and I looked into her blank white eyes.
>
> Now my lips are closed, they won't be moving,
> and I do not hear my heart's warm beat.
> I am standing on a white pedestal --
> just a statue with a bow and shield.
>
> Who am I? Athena or Diana?
> Sparkling white, illumined by the moon,
> I shall sleep -- this makes me very happy --
> seeing dreams, but only marble dreams.

Early morning. Women carry milk cans.
Autumn leaves that make the wind look brown.
Drizzling rain that sometimes comes down slanting --
such a dear, familiar Petersburg!

Suddenly... My God! A revelation:
He shall always be the one I love.
Turning into a statue could not change it --
marble lasts much longer than a heart.

There she goes. I clearly hear her singing.
My gray checkered coat is now her gain.
While I stand -- a white and unclad statue --
freezing in the autumn wind and rain.

    The first stanza already outlines the drama of two people deeply in love: the hopelessness of future encounters, the implied history of frequent meetings in which they never went beyond formal address. (I. e. they never used the familiar "thou" form in Russian [*ty*] but remained on formal, polite [*vy*] terms). His phrase: "I may never meet you here again," indicates the decision to stop seeing one another was not his; it shows uncertainty, perhaps even an anticipation of her objections. But neither tears, protest nor pleas follow. The decision is irreversible. The gates are locked. There is no exit. Apparently, the obstacles are insurmountable. Should the two of them go on as before, according to the principle "you only live once"? Should they rebel, regardless of the grief that this rebellion may cause others? For her the solution is resignation and sacrifice. It is easy to guess that she is the stronger one, yet it is not only the reader who understands her mental state after the parting. Her despair affects even one of the marble statues of the Summer Gardens. The words "blindly stumbling" could be applied to both. The words "A marble heart would never ache" confirms the thought that the statue perceives -- if not feels -- the woman's grief.

    Her readiness to cease living by exchanging places with the statue reveals the depth of this grief. Laconically, with great precision, the poet describes the scene of the exchange ("...have my shoes, my coat..."') and the outcome: ("Now my lips are closed..."'). No more heartbeat. A silent breast. A marble heart. Marble dreams. But what about memory? What about life? What about her beloved "everyday" Petersburg? Only now does she realize the immensity of the loss, and of the price she has paid for deliverance from pain. Yet is it deliverance? "Marble lasts much longer than a heart..." This line reveals more than pages of oaths and declarations of love.

The last stanza of the poem helps the reader to see the result of the transformation: one of them, the woman, standing as a statue "in the autumn wind and rain", the other walking away singing a song... It also helps us to hear the leitmotif of Odoevtseva's entire works: "How happy I feel and how sad..."

Odoevtseva's poetry was, and still is, the theme of many a thesis and critical essay by scholars and students of Slavic literature in the West and in today's Russia. It is impossible to summarize here their evaluation of her work even in short quotation. Suffice it to say that I find the article by Jacob N. Gorbov in *La Renaissance* (Paris, 1976) especially thoughtful and profound. His analysis goes to the heart of Odoevtseva's poetry. He analyses her verse collection *The Golden Chain* ("Zlataya tsep") published in Paris by "Rifma" in 1975, and perceives it as a "certain general conclusion... a starting point for poets and writers." In his opinion Odoevtseva "created a new and hitherto unknown poetic genre. Our literature of the past includes: realists, futurists, decadents, symbolists, acmeists. The poems of *The Golden Chain* do not belong to any of those categories. They are a new, very distinct one."

The critic emphasizes the "unsurpassed originality of stanzas, lines, rhymes, rhythms... and unlimited freedom of interpretation, along with the flawlessness, even mastery, of a virtuoso." He also dwells on Odoevtseva's themes, which, in his opinion, "are directly connected with the origin of her inspiration... as if she sees the human being and the world either as a miracle or as a mystery... There are two ways of approaching miracle and mystery: prayer and poetry... Odoevtseva's poetry is a perfect means of contact with the outside world."

Odoevtseva's knowledge of life was accumulated in the course of many years of creative work, encounters, partings, and reflections -- whether about the past or the future, times of consummate happiness and of abysmal grief. It was all these ingredients of life that contributed to her growth from a "little poetess with an enormous bow" into the truly great poet she became in the years of her maturity.

* * *

Selected Poems
Translated from Russian: Ella Bobrow

A notebook, some ink, my pillow,
Jasmine, the sun in a frame.
Leonora, Solveig, Liudmila,
A mermaid in waves aflame...

Thoughts of times that I loved so dearly,
Of playing life's merry game.
Of grief and its heavy hand
That weighs more than ocean sand...

* * *

Teardrops roll down the cheek from tired eyes.
Coins fall ito a brass plate, softly ringing.
Whatever prayers man sends toward the skies,
It is faith in miracles to which he is clinging.

That two times two be five,instead of four,
A stack of straw turns into a bush of roses;
And that one's castle opens all the doors,
Although there's no 'at home', just rooms and houses.

That from your grave you suddenly appear
And come towards me, alive and full of cheer.

*   *   *

To G.I.

True love. What are its laws? An idle question.
O, wonder of all wonders: wedded bliss!
There are wives in this world close to perfection;
Their kind have been and always will be -- this
Is a reality. We can't dismiss
Andromache or Penelope -- the devotion
To one's husband and submissivness to fate.
But I shall paint without exaggeration
Or ostentation a true self-portrait.

On water's surface I write declarations
Of love; I build blue castles in the air.
Yet even if you join a cloud formation,
Search stars, the moon or the beyond...Nowhere
Would you ever find a wife like me -- nowhere!

*   *   *

The Ballads

In the early twenties literary circles in Petrograd (former and later St. Petersburg) hailed the young Odoevtseva for inventing a new form of the contemporary ballad -- a form later attributed by Soviet textbooks to the Soviet poet and writer Nikolai Tikhonov. Her first work in this form, *The Ballad of Powdered Glass* ("Ballada o tolchonom stekle", 1919), created a sensation and earned the student poet a place in literary circles. Ironically, the work was rejected as a "talented failure" by Nikolai Gumilyov, her teacher at the Poetry Studio in the *Living Word Institute*. It was another poet and critic, Georgi Ivanov (later to become her husband), who first recognized the value of the work when he heard it recited at Gumilyov's house.

Gumilyov admitted his error of judgement and joined in the acclaim for his gifted student's first achievement. Others were not slow to follow. The established writer and critic Kornei Chukovsky invited Odoevtseva to inscribe her ballad in his *Chukokkala*, a personal album in which he collected the works of celebrities. Trotsky praised the poem highly, and Gorky even called it "a work of genius." On the other hand, the journal *Krasnaya zvezda* ("Red Star"), organ of the Red Army, praised the form of the work, while accusing the "stunning young poetess" of slandering the name of the Soviet Soldier.

Before emigrating from Petrograd Odoevtseva wrote several other ballads, including *The Ballad of a Coachman* ("Ballada ob izvozchike"), *The Ballad of Robert Pentague* ("Ballada o Roberte Pentague"). In all of them reality is interwoven with the fantastic. Later on, in Paris in 1923, she wrote two more: *The Ballad of Gumilyov* ("Ballada o Gumilyove") and the very short *On Place Villette* ("Na ploshchadi Villette"). I will discuss some of these poems in the pages that follow.

Despite differences in form and plot, a common element, almost a leitmotif, emerges in Odoevtseva's ballads. They are all marked by a feeling of deep compassion, not in the sense of pity, but in the much broader sense of compassion -- the presence of empathy, so characteristic of Odoevtseva's lyric poetry. We find this quality in the first lines of her *Ballad of Place Villette*. "I see the kind man go to bed / I see him kiss his wife good-night / The wicked man with jealous eye / Watches the other's house instead."

Though the author does not conceal her contempt for the wicked one, she later tries to find in his mind, perhaps only in his subconscious, signs of remorse or a wish to be different. "He dreams he's only twelve years old, / A schoolboy, merry, free of care, / He dreams, nowhere on Villette Square / A body lies, all still and cold."

At the same time the author searches for contradictory characteristics in the kind man, knowing that no one is totally kind or totally evil. She challenges the kind man's conscience: is it really that pure? "The kind man sleeps. A pallid moon / Throws sea-green light into his room,/ Yet nightmarish are all his dreams / Of jail and of the guillotine.../" But why? As the German saying has it, "A good conscience is the softest pillow."

The power of conscience and the many ways it takes its revenge, even in sleep, is the theme of *The Ballad of Powdered Glass*. The depth of insight into post-revolutionary Russia revealed by the young author in this work astonished many older, more experienced writers.

"A soldier reaches home to count / His busy day's receipts..." This man is not a profit-seeking speculator, but a soldier, to whom the Commandment "Do not kill" does not apply. He was made a soldier and taught to kill. Of course, always in the name of something or someone, always shouting: "For! or "Long live!" this, that or the other. Thus, killing for him is not a sin but a heroic deed, and his heroism is often measured by the number of killings, as in the story *The Forty First* ("Sorok pervyi") by Soviet author Boris Lavrenyov.

"Now we shall feed each hungry mouth / And meet our daily needs." Odoevtseva sees the shortage of salt in the Soviet state as an opportunity for the soldier-speculator to make thousands of rubles, and even more -- by mixing salt with powered glass. He kills without hesitation in the name of his hungry wife and children. This killing is even easier than in the war: he does not risk his own life and he will never see the dead.

In answer to his wife's cries: "...That's manslaughter... people will die!.." he calmly says: "We all must die / To harm was not my goal" and mockingly adds: "Tonight you'll go to church and buy / A candle for each soul."

Yet his wife's lament "People will die..." must have been heard and repeated over and over by his conscience. The soldier maybe hears it in the so-called "Paradise," and later at home:

"Doom... croak the carrion crows..."

"People will die... will die..." lamented the funeral bells, echoed by the wailing old women on the street: "Perhaps it is some kind of pest / No one can comprehend..." The soldier spends a sleepless night: "his double bed / Feels coffin-like and bare."

But why? After all, killing is not new to him. He has done it again "in the name of..." However, here his conscience has no justification: "A raven-priest... a glass box... upheld by seven crows." His recently awakened remorse cannot avert the punishment: thrown into a nearby gorge, he will "rot till Judgement Day".

The theme of compassion is explicit in *The Ballad of a Coachman*. The fate of the forever hungry and freezing coachman and his horse moves Odoevtseva so much that after their death she brings them into Paradise, where they will never starve or freeze -- the culmination of the coachman's dreams. In answer to St. Peter's question: "How much good did you do, when you had your choice?" the coachman describes his joyless life: "We drove the commissar every single day / To his office and home /...We starved for thirteen hundred days..." Odoevtseva makes people think about his fate and share her compassion. As the poet Osip Mandelstam once said to her: "The Petersburg coachman was always a myth. You have opened for him the gates of Paradise -- and rightly so."

In this ballad the coachman and his horse seem to live in isolation from the outside world. The commissar whom they drive daily does not care whether they are fed or starving. He notices them only when "the horse does not jerk one leg / The coachman does not crack the whip..." Even then, their death represents to him merely the loss of a service: "The coachman is dead, the horse is dead!/ Am I to run? No coachman to drive / Me to Uritsky Square number five!"

The author conveys the monotony of the coachman's life by repetition: "The coachman dozes, the coachman waits,/ The horse, too, dozes and chews./ Both always doze, both always wait..." We seem to hear the repeated cracking of the whip and the rhythmical clapping of hoofs as the tired horse slowly jogs along.

The image of the commissar is in striking contrast: "He is not young, yet shows no sign of age./ In his face there is courage, in his eyes -- a blaze.../ He pokes the coachman, he pokes the horse / And instantly leaps in -- hop!" By repeating the last two lines later in the poem, the author also evokes the contrast between the compulsive energy of the commissar and the weariness of the tired coachman.

Along with compassion there is a deep sadness permeating the *Ballad of Gumilyov*, a ballad very different from the others.

In this poem Odoevtseva truthfully relates how at Christmas of 1920 -- Gumilyov's last Christmas -- her teacher suddenly suggested she write a ballad about his life. She recalls in her memoirs how she laughingly rejected the idea that day: "Monuments are never built or ballads written for those who are still living. Perhaps, when you die, let's say in another sixty years..." Neither of them suspected then how little time remained to him. A few months later he was shot by the secret police.

Much later, while living in Paris, once the pain of losing her teacher and friend has subsided, Odoevtseva took up the theme.

"Recollections of him become sadder / Every day they slowly creep in / And now I am writing a ballad / For him and about him."

From the lines of this ballad Nikolai Gumilyov emerges not only as a poet, but also as the hero he had always wanted to be. "He faced his death in many adventures / Under deserts' alien skies..."

Odoevtseva knew before that Gumilyov had not only fearlessly hunted lions and fought with savages in Africa but had also been decorated with the St. George Cross for bravery in the First World War. Yet to her he was first and foremost a poet. Only later did she realize that "...Among the fearless ones, he was the bravest / This may be the reason why / The enemy's shells and bullets / Spared Gumilyov's life."

Between the lines of this ballad the author conveys her deep remorse at not having written about Gumilyov in his lifetime. And she openly charges his contemporaries: "The firing squad took over / They stood him against the wall / There's no cross where they buried the poet, / No grave mound, nothing at all."

Readers will notice the similarity of stanzas in the ballads *Of Powered Glass, Of Gumilyov* and *On Place Villette* (with a few exceptions in the latter). In *The Ballad of a Coachman* , Odoevtseva constructs her stanzas and chooses rhyming patterns more willfully, here rhyming three lines in a row, there leaving one line dangling without a rhyme, or elsewhere changing the pattern of quatrains altogether.

But the most unconventional of her ballads is *The Ballad of Robert Pentague*, written in 1920 and included in the anthologies *Poets' Guild* ("Tsekh poetov"), Berlin 1922, and *A Golden Chain* ("Zlataya tsep'"), Paris 1975. A Russian-American reviewer in the 70s described this ballad as "a miracle of English reincarnation... Written on the theme of a folkloric fairy tale, by the magic of poetical mastery the ballad brings old England back to life..."

The first lines of the ballad introduce the characters and their surroundings "Close to the village churchyard fence / Lives jovial grave-digger Tom / With his wife Nancy and a black tomcat." Tom likes his trade. Day after day, to the sound of church bells, he "builds for the dead a cozy home." Always alone, he is never afraid or sad. One day, "In the dusk he sees lights... On a grave mound, all still, in a row / Sit nine tomcats with their eyes aglow." Perhaps for the first time in his life as a grave-digger, Tom is frightened, for he hears a voice calling his name. Instinctively, he even takes off his hat. ("No harm in politeness even to a cat.")

Although not harmed by the cats, he is even more frightened by their message for a certain Robert Pentague, that Molly Gray has died. Tom has never heard either name before.

Later the nine cats turn into nine black-clad youths who carry a white coffin with the mysterious Molly Gray. Hearing about her death, Tom's own cat, who turns out to be Robert Pentague, jumps into the blazing fireplace.

The theme of transformation can be found quite often in the poetry of Irina Odoevtseva. So it comes as no surprise that she concludes this ballad with the lines: "I've lived through many a cat-like day / When will she die, my Molly Gray?"

*   *   *

BALLAD OF POWDERED GLASS[1]

A soldier reaches home and counts
His busy day's receipts:
"Now, we shall feed each hungry mouth
and meet our daily needs.

Five thousand rubles: this shall pass
As gain -- my lucky day!
By mixing salt and powdered glass
I added to the pay."

"My God!" his wife begins to cry,
"That's manslaughter, at least!
What have you done, people will die,
You murderer, you beast!"

The soldier says: "We all must die,
To harm was not my goal;
Tonight you'll go to church and buy
A candle for each soul."

He eats, goes out to "Paradise"
Thus is this tea-house known;
Talks of Communes, of sacrifice,
Drinks tea -- all Soviet-grown.

Three days go by. He cannot hide
The sickness of his soul;
His profit gives him no more pride,
The night falls black as coal.

---

[1] *The Ballad of Powdered Glass*, which was written in 1919 by the then very young poetess, brought her fame literally overnight. The story is based on a true occurrence in post-revolutionary Russia, when the economy was totally disrupted and even salt was sold by speculators on the black market.

He sees his house engulfed in gloom,
By midnight darkness grows.
Black wings pound at the windows... "Doom!
Doom!.." croak the carrion-crows.

The children, hearing thumps and cries,
Look pale and terrified.
The soldier's wife laments and sighs,
But he sleeps through the night.

Awake, he's angry; fear creeps in,
He feels depressed and sore.
His wife keeps praying for his sin,
Her forehead on the floor.

"Get out of town! Go, find a bowl,
There you can say your prayers.
I'm sick and tired, dammit all,
Of powdered glass affairs!"

Alone, he play the gramophone,
Relaxes in a chair.
Then... Funeral bells. A distant drone...
He shakes, turns pallid. There!..

There! Seven coffins -- what a load!
And seven jades that haul
Them on a cart along the road...
Old women sob and howl.

"Say, Konstantin, who passed away
"Our sister Glasha's gone;
Came from a party on Thursday,
Got sick and died at dawn.

Nick's father-in-law, too, is at rest,
Fomá, Klim, found their end;
Perhaps, it is some kind of pest
No one can comprehend."

The soldier meets the night with dread.
The moon comes out to stare.
He tries to sleep, his double bed
Feels coffin-like and bare.

A raven-priest... Perhaps he dreams,
The scene is too morose;
A glass-box follows -- so it seems --
Upheld by seven crows.

They fill the corners, standing there --
A black and frightful mass.
"Shoo, devils! Should I live, I swear
I'll never sell powdered glass!"

Too late. No one comes to his aid.
The seven crows come near,
Their priest croaks seven times, they lay
The corpse into the bier.

They carry him to a gorge nearby,
Filled up with foul decay.
They throw him in with scorn to lie
And rot till Judgement Day.

* * *

BALLAD OF A COACHMAN

At the house on sixty Basin Street
Stops a coachman every single day.
He takes the commissar to the commissariat:
The commissar likes the easy way.

The coachman dozes, the coachman waits,
The horse, too, dozes and chews.
Both always doze, both always wait --
The commissar is due at the commissariat.

The commissar Zon appears at last,
Approaches the coachman, walks lightly, fast.
He is not young, yet shows no sign of age.
In his face there is courage, in his eyes a blaze --
That's the commissar with his special ways.
He pokes the coachman, he pokes the horse,
And instantly leaps in, hop!

The coachman pulls the rein,
The horse jerks one leg;
The coachman says: "Let's go, old rogue!"
The horse lifts up one leg,

Then puts it on the ground again --
The coach rolls slightly back.
The coachman cracks the whip,
They're off on their daily trip.

The tired horse slowly jogs along,
At five the coachman sets out for home.
He heads for the tea house to have some tea,
His horse, while waiting, chews some hay.

But the door of the tea house is locked.
There is a sign: "Closed on account of logs."[2]
The coachman sighs: "Oh, what the heck!"
He sighs again, scratching his neck.
The tired horse slowly jogs along,
The hungry coachman sets out for home.

---

[2] A grammatically incorrect phrase used by Odoevtseva for its comic effect. Literally: closed because of logs ("Zakryto po sluchayu drov").

Next morning -- it is a cloudy day --
He stops at sixty Basin Street
To take the commissar to the commissariat;
The commissar likes the easy way.
The commissar Zon appears at last,
Approaches the coachman, walks lightly, fast.
He pokes the coachman, he pokes the horse
And instantly leaps in, hop!

But the coachman does not pull the rein,
His horse does not move a leg,
The coachman does not crack the whip,
They do not start their tedious trip.
The commissar shouts: "O, hell, what's that?
The coachman is dead, the horse is dead!
Am I to run? No coachman to drive
Me to Uritsky Square number five!"

Above, on the heaven's light blue way
The coachman walks with his horse one day.
They arrive at the gates of paradise:
"Won't you open for us, Saint Peter, please!"
Through the closed door sounds Saint Peter's voice:
"How much good did you do when you had your
      choice?"
"We drove the commissar every single day
To his office and home; don't turn us away.
We starved for thirteen hundred days
Do have mercy on me and my horse!
Here in paradise, we won't starve or freeze,
Open for me and my poor horse, please!"

Apostle Peter came out at last.
He looked at the horse: "What a wretched beast!
Well, then, step in, what can I say?"
The two entered Eden to stay.

*   *   *

BALLAD OF ROBERT PENTAGUE

Close to the village churchyard fence
Lives jovial grave-digger Tom
with Nancy his wife
And a black tomcat.

Whenever church bells slowly toll,
God has recalled another soul.
Digging a grave, the jovial Tom
Builds for the dead a cozy home.

One winter day, he was at work. The sun
Approached the horizon and soon was gone.
Though all alone, Tom was not afraid,
He had come to like the grave-digger's trade.
When the work was done, the hour was late,
Tom headed for home, content with fate.
Then in the dusk, he saw lights -- a long row,
Almost like tiny church-candles aglow.
"God be with me," whispered Tom. Then the sound
Of a voice: "Hey, Tom!" He turned, looked around...
On a fresh grave mound, all still, in a row
Sat nine tomcats with their eyes aglow.

Tom, startled, shouted: "Who's calling me?"
"Me-I," answered one cat somberly.
Tom quickly took off his hat;
No harm in politeness, even to a cat.
"Anything, sir, I could do for you?.."
"Would you, please, tell Robert Pentague
About the death of Molly Gray.
Keep calm, we won't harm you in any way!"
Then, wildly mewing, in a great rush
The cats disappeared in the underbrush.

Nancy spun and waited for Tom patiently,
In the corner their cat purred sleepily.

Then Tom dashed in, shouting: "What should I do,
Nancy, help me, who is Molly Gray?
I'm supposed to tell Robert Pentague
That she passed away yesterday.
But who is this Robert Pentague,
And where do I find him? I wish I knew."
From the corner, their cat sprung out and cried:
"Did you say Molly Gray has died?!
Farewell, be happy, may God bless you!"
And into the blazing fire he flew.

Ping-dong! Ping-dong-dong!
The church-bells lamented all morning long.
On the street ten black-capped youths appeared
On their shoulders they bore a snow-white bier.
"Whom do they bury? Who are those ten?"
Tom asked the churchyard-verger Sam.
"No one here knows her, but some do say
That her name was Molly Gray.

I wouldn't know, who are those youths
And I don't care, to tell the truth."
Sam shrugged and spat, Tom felt a chill,
Recalled the tomcats, yet kept still.

I remember hearing this tale oft-told
In my childhood; it charmed my mind and soul
Forever; because I, too,
Am in a strange way Robert Pentague.
I've lived through many a cat-like day,

When will she die, my Molly Gray?

* * *

BALLAD OF GUMILYOV

In deserted Preobrazhensky
Snow was driven by a howling wind.
When I knocked (I was shy, apprehensive),
Gumilyov himself let me in.

Burning wood added cheer to his study,
Skies grew darker, the night was near.
Gumilyov said: "You could write a ballad
About my whole life, about me.

It is really an excellent subject."
But I laughingly answered: "No!
You are a poet, you are not a hero,
How would I start? I wouldn't know."

He kept still, but a fleeting sadness
For a moment changed his face.
On a misty Petersburg Christmas
Eve, this meeting took place.

Recollections of him become sadder
Every day. They slowly creep in.
And now I am writing a ballad
For him and about him.
Gumilyov sailed down the Bosphorus
To Africa's wonderland,
Thinking of ancient heroes
Under the sky's vast tent.

Here and there, like thin threads of fire,
Shooting stars kept falling down.
He longingly begged of each star:
"Bring me a hero's crown!"

For half a year he lived in a desert
Under a singular spell;
Shot lions, joined battles with natives
In this long coveted hell.

He faced death in many adventures,
Under deserts' alien skies.
Later, back home, in Russia
Friends poked fun at him many times:

"Ah, Africa! Did you enjoy it?
Camp-fires, dark beauties, tom-toms...
Are all giraffes refined and haughty?
Is your friend hippo second to none?"

He went to a formal reception
In tails, looking diffident;
Met a lady in a gown from Paris
And gallantly kissed her hand:

"Just for you I will write a poem,
To tell you about the Nile;
I will give you the leopard skin trophy
For which I once risked my life."

The pink fan swayed in rejection:
"I need no wild animal skin,
I read poems just on occasion."
She was clearly not fond of him.

And then, when the World War started,
Gumilyov went away to fight.
Went away, leaving in Tsarskoye
His mother, his son, his wife.

Among the fearless ones, he was the bravest.
This may be the reason why
The enemy's shells and bullets
Spared Gumilyov's life.

But for his St. George's Crosses,
Some friends had a scornful sneer.
Their remarks offhandedly caustic:
"Gumilyov and a Cross? That's rare!

Those cavalry-private's Crosses
Are nothing -- a dime for three!
He goes with his friends at Headquarters
On many a drinking spree."

...Once, before death, he boasted
In jest, full of confidence: "Yes!
In love, war, and cards -- I will always
Look upon Fortune's face.

I'm calm when my life is threatened,
Danger to me is a farce..."
And yet he was very unhappy,
Unhappy as all poets are.

The firing squad took over:
They stood him against the wall.
There's no cross where they buried the poet,
No grave mound, nothing at all.

But his favourite seraphs came flying
To claim the poet's soul.
In heaven the stars were singing:
"Hail to you, Hero, Hail!"

*   *   *

ON PLACE VILLETTE

I see the kind man go to bed,
I see him kiss his wife good night.
The wicked man with a jealous eye
Watches the other's house instead.

He's evil-minded. Yesterday,
Perhaps, he forged a plan to steal.
Tomorrow he might take away
The life of any man at will.
Then he, a killer and a thief,
Would clean his knife on a blood-stained sleeve.

The kind man sleeps. A pallid moon
Throws sea-green light into his room.
Yet nightmarish are all his dreams
Of jails and of the guillotine.
Still half asleep, he'd loudly cry,
Fighting the man who made him die.

The wicked man sits in the bar
At leisure, he enjoys his wine
And broods on a future dark design.
At night sound sleep is his reward.
He dreams he's only twelve years old,
A schoolboy, merry, free of care,

He dreams, nowhere on Villette Square
A body lies, all still and cold.

* * *

Irina Odoevtseva's Short Prose

As mentioned in our chapter *On the Banks of the Seine*, Odoevtseva's first short story *A Shooting Star* ("Paduchaya zvezda") enjoyed great success in Russian émigré literary circles. So much so that Ivan Bunin, doyen of émigré literature, wrote a note to the publisher of *Latest News* ("Poslednie novosti"), expressing praise and a desire to meet the author of the story. The meeting took place in 1926. Unfortunately, the work itself now proves impossible to find.

A Shooting Star evidently dealt with the life of a Russian émigré woman who is being persuaded to return to the Soviet Union, but decides to remain in the West, despite the unhappy circumstances of her personal life.

In the middle of the twenties the question of whether to remain or to return tormented the soul of many a Russian émigré. The inner conflict of the heroine who longed for "her" Russia was thus familiar to Russian readers. Yet clearly it was not only its popular plot that made *A Shooting Star* a success. It was Odoevtseva's masterly treatment of it that aroused the enthusiasm of readers and critics. We can find indirect evidence of this by referring to an episode with a similar theme in her novel *The Mirror* ("Zerkalo") published fifteen years later, in 1939. Eleven of its pages are dedicated to another Russian émigré woman. This time she is a movie star, who is pregnant, in love with and loved by her director, yet rejected by him for superstitious reasons. We meet her on the train to Paris after their stormy encounter in Venice. She is shattered to the point of contemplating suicide. A Russian tourist from the Soviet Union shares the compartment with her. He observes her and is full of admiration for her beauty and compassion for her grief. Sensing his sympathy, she opens her heart to him and tells him all about her life, recounting her childhood, her recent great happiness in love, and her present deep despair.

Odoevtseva purposely leaves the Russian character in the shade. He remains merely a compassionate listener who tries to calm and console "Lyukushka", as he already calls her.

In answer to her hopeless question "What should I do now?" he suggests she consider a future as a movie actress in Moscow. She is stunned by this solution. "How perfectly simple... This morning she didn't even know this man... Yet now he takes her hand and leads her along the familiar snow-covered streets of Moscow... Why hadn't she thought of this possibility before herself?.. Now they both make plans on a global scale, plans for Lyuka, future star of the Russian screen..."

Although this novel was written during Stalin's merciless purges, ideology never enters their conversation. Lyuka is too occupied with herself -- at first with the dramatic turn in her life, then with plans for her future. But the reader understands the Russian tourist's words before his departure for Moscow: "You are talking about your unhappiness and I sympathize with your sorrow. But I still cannot fully believe in it... your grief is like that in some operetta, it's not real..." As the two of them part, the man again advises her to contact the Soviet Embassy, but he does not give her his full name and address in Moscow. "These are not times for correspondence with abroad..."

Alone once more, the heroine again sees all their plans for the future as an illusion. "Why go to Moscow and not to the moon?.. Anguish, like an ember from hellfire, burned in her heart... Hopes for Moscow were already reduced to ashes. How still... like after some great conflagration. Everything is destroyed, and the flame dies in the ashes and its soul like a thin, touchingly pathetic stripe rises to heaven. Yet this lasted only a moment. Having finished with the future and the present, her anguish now attacked the past. But that past was made of ferroconcrete, fireproof. The past would not burn.

If the lost story of *A Shooting Star* was written with the same poetic and passionate pen as this episode, one can understand why Russian readers of the twenties welcomed Irina Odoevtseva as an original prose writer. However, she soon turned to the genre of the novel, then to memoirs. There was no more time for short stories. Besides, even in her prose she remained a poet. A language saturated with poetic images and an ability to captivate the reader's mind with a fascinating plot -- these were the secrets of the success of her prose.

And whether we think of the little girl misunderstood and rejected by her self-centered young stepmother ("Valentine"), or the "talking" dachshund who helped its owner regain her will to live ("Eric"), or the boy who suffered because there was no love and peace between his parents (*Dry Straw* -- "Sukhaya soloma"), -- in all of these works, by penetrating her characters' inner world, hidden from view, Irina Odoevtseva compels her reader to believe in them, to share their feelings and understand their psychological conflicts.

Actually Odoevtseva never stopped writing short stories. We find many of them scattered over the pages of her memoirs. Suffice it to mention only a few of the most memorable ones: the story of Georgi Ivanov's childhood; Sologub's Golden Tower and his unsuccessful attempts to emigrate to the West; Bunin's "kindest deed" and his graveyard story; the turbulent relationship of Blok and Bely -- a story of friendship, nobility, love, betrayal and repentance; Kuzmin's asceticism and subsequent return to a "sinful" life... There are many other episodes much shorter but not less memorable. There are even more humorous stories in miniature contained in the volume of her memoirs, especially in the sections about Osip Mandelstam.

All these latter stories seem even more valuable than the invented ones, since they not only excite and move us, make us laugh, capture our imagination: they also bring to life

Odoevtseva's contemporaries, and help us to remember them forever.

As a courageous innovator, Odoevzeva uses all available genres originally and willfully -- now interweaving them, now using them to complement each other. Yet her stories, novels and memoirs are always triumphantly dominated by poetry.

* * *

The Angel of Death
("Angel Smerti")

This novel, Irina Odoevtseva's first, appeared in 1927 in the daily paper *Dni* (Days). Later it was not only published in book form, but also reissued -- a rarity for an émigré writer's work. The novel has also been translated into seven foreign languages. The English version, by Donia Nanchen (*Constable*, N.Y., 1930) was printed four times under the title *Out of Childhood*, and won an award as the best translated novel of the year. Unfortunately, copyright was erroneously ascribed to the translator, and Odoevtseva did not protest the matter in law.

The Angel of Death was a great critical success, not only in Russian literary circles but also in English ones. The émigré journal *Dates* ("Chisla") published excerpts from more than a dozen favourable reviews in English press. Reviewers, including those from such influential publications as the *Manchester Guardian* and the *New Statesman*, praised the book for its delicacy, tenderness, conciseness of means, and beauty of expression. The work was compared to Chekhov and hailed as a triumph, as one of the important events of the literary season.

Such reviews inevitably arouse modern readers' curiosity about this book which sold out half a century ago and is now available in very few libraries. What makes this novel so singular?

Recounting the plot is both easy and difficult. The novel contains little action and, as in any work of art, its power lies not in its choice of subject, but in the author's masterful handling of it. What makes *The Angel of Death* special is Odoevtseva's skill in blending subtle images to create living characters.

Lyuka, a 14-year-old girl with an ardent imagination, is eager to grow up as quickly as possible. She is secretly in love with Arseniy, an admirer of her beautiful older sister Vera. Wishful thinking convinces her that Arseniy visits their house only for her, Lyuka's, sake, but he does not reveal his love only because she is still too young, and he therefore uses Vera as a coverup.

Vera marries a wealthy man and is expecting a child. Arseniy, who has rented a cottage in the neighbourhood, visits the family frequently. Lyuka suffers from what she believes is his feigned coldness. But one day, knowing he is away from home, she enters his cottage and finds on the desk an unfinished letter. "My dear little girl, I've spent another day in your house without being able to tell you how much I love you. It torments me. Your mother, your sister..."

Now she is sure that he has been in love with her for a long time and is only waiting for her to grow up. But am I not going to be fifteen soon, she thinks, and didn't mother recently say that I'm already a big girl?

So one night she puts on her sister's dress, goes to him, and confesses that she now knows from his unfinished letter about his love for her. When he asks why she came, she wistfully answers: "I thought when people are in love, they always want to be together at night."

Fearing that the girl will reveal his secret love for her sister Vera, Arseniy forces her to swear to keep silent about her love for him. He calms her down with tender kisses and does not dispel her mistaken belief. Lyuka experiences the happiness she had dreamed about in those mysterious, languid, stifling nights.

Outwardly nothing changes in the following days; Arseniy continues to pay more attention to Vera. But Lyuka is happy; she now knows the joy of his tenderness and waits eagerly for their next encounter, not suspecting its tragic consequences.

One day Vera finds Arseniy on his knees before Lyuka in the pavilion. Enraged and horrified, she shrinks back, falls from the stairs and dies in premature childbirth. In her delirium she curses Lyuka and Arseniy for causing her death.

The heroine of the novel is, of course, the girl Lyuka. Through her eyes the author sees the small world in which the adult characters around her live, love, and suffer. The author does not describe them. Instead the reader learns details of them gradually through Lyuka's observations and contemplations. Thus we hear about Lyuka's father's death from a scene in which Vera reproaches her mother for competing with her at a ball and dancing too often with Vera's admirers: "You should at least remember that father has been shot by the Bolsheviks."

Vera's nature is somewhat confusing, full of contradictions. She is often abrupt and makes hard-hearted remarks. Even her mother muses: "You're strange. Though at times you're affectionate, you have no heart. And you don't love any one. You're like a cat." Her mother is especially shocked at Vera's cold indifference when a former lover of her then fiancé attempts suicide: "Had she really poisoned herself, she'd have died... let's not talk about her... let her live, I don't mind."

Later, softened by pregnancy, she cries while reading an old newspaper clipping about an Arab, now condemned to death, who had been so poor as a child that he used to eat grass. "Mother... I can't help it... I feel so sorry for him." This is no longer the self-centred Vera, interested only in preserving her own beauty, who screams hysterically on learning of her pregnancy: "I don't want it... I'd rather die... This is horrible, repulsive, ugly..."

Using short brush strokes, the author reveals the changes in Vera's nature as motherhood approaches. She no longer looks down on her younger sister Lyuka. ("You're foolish... When will you get smarter?") Now she often affectionately calls her "chicken", and even decides to name her future child (it must be a girl!) Lyudmila, "so that she will be as merry and pretty as my Lyuka."

In spite of being heavier now, Vera feels light and happy, with no more fear, rage or sadness. "The closer the time, the lighter... Each day now is a holiday, each one counts. Does anyone know how many are left?... But she feels no fear, not at all, except at night..." Of course, there is another reason for her elevated mood: Arseniy's frequent visits. Her hope that she would in time grow fond of her husband does not materialize. Vera is so happy that she doesn't object to Arseniy going for a walk with Lyuka. For a while she enjoys being alone, dreaming about her little girl and sewing a tiny blouse for her. But then she feels the baby moving, and decides to look for Arseniy and tell him about it. It is at this point that she finds him on his knees before Lyuka. "Vera suddenly steps back... and leans with all her weight upon the banister. The last thing she sees, unbearably blue and glasslike, is the sky above her head. Then suddenly the sky cracks. Huge pieces of blue glass, ringing and rattling, fall to the earth and crash down upon Vera..."

She loses her child and dies, never knowing that Lyuka had been unaware of Arseniy's real feelings and of Vera's love for him. Before Vera dies, she repents her illicit love affair. Now she wants her girl to have not dark eyes like her lover's, but light eyes like her husband's -- "just like yours, Volodya... You, she and I. We shall be swimming and she will lie there on the sand in the sun..."

One of the assertions of the great drama teacher Stanislavsky was: when playing a villain, show him in a moment of kindness. Odoevtseva's heroes are real, and we remember them because both their virtues and their vices are presented to us.

The girls' mother is a kind, unhappy woman, widowed early and still beautiful. She takes care of her appearance but not, as Vera charges, in order to find a husband. Rather, her main concern is Vera -- Lyuka, still a teenager, has lots of time, so her mother thinks. Vera's unhappy marriage, her love for another man, her horror at motherhood, and finally her tragic death break the mother both physically and spiritually. At Vera's funeral Lyuka finds herself looking at an old woman with a pale, swollen face, and wonders if this can really be her mother.

In this novel the men play secondary roles -- as cause of joy or suffering for the female characters. Thus we learn very little about Vera's husband. He is respected at his plant. He must be rather well off, since Lyuka notices his gold watch and cigarette case. He loves Vera passionately and blindly, not seeing or not wanting to see her faults. Fearing to lose her, he forgives her abruptness, her indifference, even her unfaithfulness. When told about her pregnancy, he whispers, bewildered: "But... I don't understand how could it have happened." His protest goes no further.

Vera's mother enlightens us with a remark about Arseniy: "He spends money too freely for someone who doesn't work anywhere... I've heard he has an old American woman in Paris..." One can only guess that this is one of his reasons for not marrying Vera; he is in love with her, yet avoids the responsibilities of a husband and father. Nevertheless, the reader is convinced that his love for her and his grief at her sudden death are sincere.

But let us take a further look at Lyuka, who unknowingly causes the tragic outcome. Who is she, this girl "in love with love", outwardly mischievous and merry, who in a fit of ecstasy could "shake out the down from all the pillows... like Chaplin."

In self-defence, Lyuka will quite readily challenge another girl at school to a boxing match. When her shocked mother asks how girls can fight, Lyuka answers: "You were only silk dolls at your Institute. We just hit one another with our fists. We box and try to hit one another on the jaw or punch one another in the stomach, although it's forbidden." Lyuka can also swing gracefully and skilfully on a trapeze, and people often say about her: "Lyuka is merry and fearless, she should be a boy."

Lyuka admires Vera's beauty without being envious, although she talks back and at times upsets her with her mischievous pranks. But these are the visible traits of Lyuka the little girl. Like all Odoevtseva's heroines, Lyuka is many-sided.

A puritanical reader would call her dissolute or immoral in trying to seduce Arseniy. Here she is with him at a waterfall, to which they have ridden on a motorcycle:
"You are going away tomorrow... I'm sad..." she sobbed loudly.
Arseniy looked embarrassed: "Stop it... dear little Lyuka."
"Kiss me, and I'll stop crying." He leant over and lightly kissed her cheek.
"No, not that way. On the lips, or I'll start crying again."
"You are crazy," he said, frightened, and kissed her childish lips, salty with tears.
"Again and again. Embrace me... I'm not crazy, I'm only grown up, but you all treat me like a child."
"Of course," he agreed, afraid to contradict her. "You are a grown up."
She sighed deeply and cuddled up closer to him. "Kiss me once more..."
"We must go back home, they'll be worried," he meekly said.
"Yes, we must, because I left home secretly... But kiss me again. Listen, you yourself said I'm grown up. Tonight I'll wait for you in my room. You'll come into the garden, I'll climb out through the window..." Later, riding home on Arseniy's motorcycle, Lyuka shouts: "I'll wait. You must come. Promise..."
"Stop talking, hold your tongue."
Lyuka waits at her open window until dawn, thinking: "He'll come. He must come..." But he does not come. Lyuka sleeps in, and nearly misses Arseniy's departure. Shaking her hand, he says: "Grow up to be big and clever... In Paris some day we'll definitely go to the circus to see the lions." The next day she is in bed, "sick with grief and love" (and with a severe cold after her night by the open window). She does not get up for a month. After her illness she looks thinner and taller. She keeps thinking about Arseniy day and night, though waiting becomes more and more difficult -- after all, she *is* his fiancée...

A romantic reader might see Lyuka in a very different light: as a girl with a poetic soul, a mind inclined to dream, a rich imagination, a girl who yearns to become an adult and to be loved. By just closing her eyes, this girl could be back in Russia. "How can one forget?.. St. Petersburg... white, pure, glistening snow. Everything is white and shiny. The streets, the roofs, the air. The bright blue sky with the huge, frosty, rosy sun. Along the wide, straight snow-covered avenues, horses race and red-cheeked coachmen shout: Beware! Ladies wearing sable or ermine coats are driven in graceful little sleighs. On the sidewalks officers promenade, trailing their sabres and tinkling their spurs... They wear brass helmets decorated with swinging horsetails..." Lyuka imagines herself on the Neva where "On the blue ice tiny elves glide on silver skates..."

Lyuka does not want to part with her poetic image of real life. Thus she is disgusted when her girl friends Yvonne and Jeanne describe their sexual experiments with their cousin Paul. When Jeanne starts to tell her that she knows not only how to make babies, but also how to prevent this, Lyuka screams: "Don't you dare, I don't want to hear... Shut up!" She covers her ears and runs away. But at night she sees mysterious dreams that are horrifying and enrapturing at the same time. During the day she repeats the verses: "There comes an Angel of Death in the threatening hour of last torments and final parting. He holds us close in his embrace, yet very cold are all his kisses." She remembers the rustle of his black wings, the brilliance of his black eyes. She feels the touch of his light cold hands... Azrael... She waits eagerly for the night and another dream so "blissful, light, and terrifying."

When her down-to-earth sister one night switches on the light and forces Lyuka to listen to the explanation of those vague half-dreams, the girl almost falls ill: "Everything is clear, coarse, repulsive, terrible. And how can people go on living, how can one -- if this is true?..." After this scene, Azrael no longer appears in her dreams.

But Lyuka's romantic soul continues to dream about Arseniy's imaginary love. She knows -- or has convinced herself

-- that she has known him since childhood. He was the dark-eyed elf with whom she used to ride in a sleigh on the blue ice of the Neva; it was with him that she waltzed on the parquet of a brightly lit ballroom. And later they were in a room filled with flowers. There the elf said: "I love you, Lyuka... I'll marry you when you grow up... My name is Arseniy. And you must wait for me."

Now, finally, her dreams are reality. She has read his letter; she confesses that she waited for him. But when she begins to write to Jeanne about her happiness, she reflects on the events of the night before. "How could it be described?.. Actually nothing has happened... It's different from what Vera told her about..."

Still, everything around her has changed. It is a completely new Lyuka who returns from her visit to Arseniy. In this mood she awaits another encounter -- one that finally opens her eyes.

We part with the girl Lyuka at her sister's funeral. The author will tell us about the fate of Lyuka as a married woman twelve years later in the novel *The Mirror*, which is discussed in another chapter of this book.

In conclusion, we must mention the language of Odoevtseva's first novel. It is the language of a poet. It is impossible to quote all the lines or the whole pages that have the ring of poetry. Even in the usually sober Vera's speech we find many poetic lines, especially in her contemplations. As for Lyuka -- all her dreams, daydreams and recollections remind us, more than anything else, of the poetry of Odoevtseva, who even in her prose never ceased to be a poet.

*   *   *

The following are some excerpts from reviews of *The Angel of Death* published in Russian by the émigré periodical *Chisla* in 1927.

"It is difficult to define the most beautiful aspect of this book, rare in its beauty. Its tenderness and delicacy remind us of Katherine Mansfield's most airy, transparent stories." (*Manchester Guardian*)

"This is a novel about youth filled with dreams, horror, enchantment, rare delight. It is very light and extremely meaningful... Odoevtseva has created a work of unforgettable beauty." (*New Statesman*)

"Odoevtseva's book carries the unmistakable mark of genius. We even dare to put it on the same level with Chekhov. No praise of this book seems to us exaggerated." *(Gastonia Gazette)*

"A complete theme has been treated with admirable tenderness and fineness, giving this book the quality of timelessness." *(Birmingham Post)*

"One cannot find words to describe the refined and enchanting fragrance of this novel. The book is very cleverly and interestingly constructed. Each phrase is full of tragic meaning." *(The Times)*

"The reader is torn between compassion for both heroines. Their tragedy leaves a bitter taste after having read the last page. This is a book one can't forget." *(Saturday Night)*

"Odoevtseva's book is one of the outstanding events of the American book season... It is one of the best books translated from Russian for the last decade." *(Cannonsburg Notes)*

"...This story of a tragedy of youth is recounted extremely delicately... Despite the conciseness of means the characters are true to life. Odoevtseva's writing makes things that could seem disgusting sound refined and beautiful..." *(Evening Post, Chicago)*

"A fascinating, unique, highly artistic book. A document that is sinister and at the same time full of memorable charm. One of the few real events in the world of books." *(B.Monical)*

* * *

Isolde ("*Isolda*")

There is nothing unusual in the plot of this novel, except for the characters' ages; at first reading it may seem to be a detective story. The wealthy English youth Cromwell falls in love with the 14-year-old Russian girl Liza. Her brother Kolya and his friend Andrei take advantage of this situation. They persuade Cromwell to rob his mother for a noble cause. Then they kill him in order to use the jewellery for their own purposes. Deceived and originally ignorant of their real plan, Liza realizes that she has been an unwitting accomplice in the crime. She decides to die with Andrei whom she loved, like the legendary Isolde and Tristan.

This novel, which appeared in 1929, two years after *The Angel of Death* ("Angel Smerti"), aroused the most contradictory responses, from severe censure to enthusiastic praise. Milyukov, editor of the *Latest News*, ("Poslednie Novosti"), concluded: "it is time to tell this young gifted writer that she has reached a dead end". There were heated public debates: some called the novel immoral, accusing the author of slandering Russian émigré youth; others defended the novel's artistic value. The critic Chervinsky once exclaimed indignantly: "Have I lost my mind or have you?.. Don't you realize what a wonderful novel this is?"

Jacob N. Gorbov, the famed Russian-French writer and editor, was so enthralled by the artistry of *Isolde* that he carried the novel with him to the front in 1940 and kept rereading it while in hospital. It was in 1960 that he met Odoevtseva. She had his ragged copy hardbound and returned it to its owner with a touching inscription.

In his thoughtful and highly laudatory review of the novel Gorbov wrote: "This book is remarkable and terrifying. Once you start reading, you can't put it down. The fact that the crime is committed by very young people... makes it not merely a detective novel... In this respect Odoevtseva has reached the level of writers like Conan Doyle... She describes her characters tersely yet compellingly."

Since *Isolde* is by now a bibliographical rarity and thus unobtainable for the majority of readers, I would like to demonstrate the reasons for the critics' heated admiration or indignation. This is best done not by recounting the novel, but by attempting to penetrate into the hearts and minds of the characters.

Odoevtseva draws the portraits of her protagonists with a very fine brush. We are never given a full description. Rather, the characters come alive to the reader gradually -- through their actions, conversations, and above all through their thoughts or meditations. As in all truly artistic works, their deeds are a logical consequence of their natures, and the reader believes that a given character could act in no other way. As the reader comes, step by step, to know a character, however, initial impressions shift. Thus, in the first two parts of the novel, Liza/ Isolde may not appear likeable to the reader, especially to parents of young girls -- this even now, half a century later, after Nabokov's Lolita and similar "nymphettes" have become heroines of a whole series of novels and films.

We first meet Liza on the beach in Biarritz, alone. A girl has drowned and Liza is shaken. She obediently lets herself be led away from the site of the accident by an unknown youth. They sit down on the sand and she, in a quiet voice, starts the conversation.

"Are you English? I am Russian. What's your name?"
"Cromwell."
"Cromwell? That's in honour of *the* Cromwell?", she asked, recalling and pointing backward with her hand, as though past centuries dwelt somewhere there behind her shoulder.
"Yes, in honour of him."
"Your parents must have known history well?"
"I suppose so." He smiled. "And what is your name?"
"Mine? Liza."
He shook his head. "No, your name is Isolde."
"Isolde? Who was that?"
He handed her a book. "Here, there's something written about you. Read it."
"About me?" She opened the book and read the title: Tristan and Isolde.
"No," she remarked quietly. "This is not about me. Isolde was a queen. But I'll read the book. Thanks.
No, I am not a queen," she repeated. "And I'm very modern. Why are you staring at me like that?"
"Go on and change your clothes. It's turning cooler. You'll catch a cold."
He suddenly panicked, afraid of losing her. "I'll wait for you.
What are you doing this evening? Is anybody waiting for you?"
"No, but I'll go home for dinner. I am very hungry."
"But if nobody is waiting for you, you can dine with me. Let's go.
My car is here."
"A car? Your own?"
"Yes. That was my spring present for the exams."
"What make?"
"A Buick."
"A Buick," she repeated and laughed obviously pleased. His own Buick. "I'll be with you right away."
I have taken the liberty of introducing such a long quotation not only to illustrate the laconic style of conversation, but

also to indicate Odoevtseva's subtle ability to reveal characters. From this fragment we learn that Liza does not have strict parents; nobody waits for her; she can dispose of her time at will. She is impressed by wealth. She is not afraid to go off with a stranger and accepts his invitation without embarrassment.
We also learn something about Cromwell. He is romantic, ready to idealize Liza by seeing her as Isolde. He is surprised that she smokes; he is modest, a good student and, apparently, the son of wealthy parents. And he is not afraid to express his disapproval:
"No, you are not Isolde. And since you put on make up, your loose hair is not becoming."
She blushed. "You don't like me? Give me your handkerchief." She quickly wiped off her lips. "You are an Englishman, a puritan, a Quaker." She laughed. "But let it be. I want you to like me. Is this better?"
But since I am neither English nor puritan, I follow the two of them in Cromwell's automobile in my mind and I observe Isolde with increasing alarm. I must confess that she continues to shock me. Judge for yourself. Let us allow her and the author to speak again (in this book, in which every phrase is full of significance, any passage is revealing).

... The wind tossed her long hair.
"I can't see the road. We'll break our necks because of your long hair. Please, don't take it away, I beg you. It smells good."
Liza was laughing quietly. "It smells of sea-water. I am so happy. I'm not afraid."
Her knee was touching his. She leaned her head on his shoulder...
"So, where are we going?" he asked.
"I don't know. Not to a restaurant. Listen, would you like to go to the lighthouse? People in love always go to the lighthouse. And you *are* in love with me, aren't you?"
He looked at her seriously.
"Yes, I am in love with you, Isolde."

"You really love me? How nice, I am so glad." Her face became thoughtful, almost sad. "But, you know, if you love me, I must tell you. I already have a friend. At present he is in Paris."
Cromwell moved away. "Oh, so that's it."
But Lisa quickly took his hand. "No, you misunderstood me, it doesn't mean anything. You can be in love with me. I like you very much."
She looked at him timidly.
"Kiss me."
He shook his head.
"But it doesn't mean anything. You are so naïve. It's so nice to kiss." She embraced his neck. "Kiss me, please."
The automobile stopped. Liza again asks him to kiss her and not to be angry with her. When he finally bends over and does so, she sighs deeply and says, closing her eyes: "I only wanted you to know that I'm no longer a child." Perhaps this last sentence is meant to explain her daring approach to the strange young man. Next morning, when her brother asks her how late she stayed out, she says:
"Not late at all. Besides you would approve of the way I spent the evening. You can congratulate me -- I have my own automobile."
"Where from?"
"A wealthy Englishman fell in love with me. He owns a Buick. And if he owns one, so do I. He's rich. You should see how much money he carries in his wallet."
"You're not lying, are you, Liza?"
"No. I'll introduce you to him, if you'll be nice. Don't mention it to 'her'."
Only now do we learn that Liza and Kolya still have a mother, but she in fact poses as their cousin and wants to be called Natasha. She sings in the "Chateau Basque" and tries to look younger than her age. Much later we find out more about her life from Liza's reflections. She is the widow of a former Russian navy officer who was killed by sailors after the revolu-

tion -- a detail that helps one to understand the tragedy of her life. In Constantinople she used to work in a restaurant; in Paris, in a store. The temptations of a merry, festive life have led her to take up with a wealthy "uncle." But neither gambling nor a change of admirers have brought real happiness. Her present lover, Boris, uses her in various occasional schemes involving blackmail and deceit. The victim in this case is Abram V. Rokhlin, nicknamed "Krolik" (Rabbit) by Kolya and Liza. Their mother despises him, but knowing that he is married to a wealthy woman, she is willing to extort money from him, to give to Boris.

She tries unsuccessfully to hide these goings-on from her children. They are not deceived, but are no doubt psychologically affected by her way of life. Liza likes to be admired and entertained. Kolya thinks only about money for gambling and luxury and speaks cynically about their mother and her admirers. She herself is often away on extended trips, yet she doesn't allow her children to call her "mother", not even in letters.

When one reads *Isolde* after *The Angel of Death*, one cannot help comparing the way of life of the novels' characters, and consequently their actions.

Liza, like Lyuka in *The Angel of Death*, is a young girl under fifteen. Both were orphaned in Russia after the revolution and raised in France. Each has her own secret world, open only to the reader. The dream of being loved occupies most of their thoughts. Liza's mother devotes even less time to her daughter than does Lyuka's mother, although for different reasons.

Yet, in spite of the similarities of family environment and circumstances, the girls grow and develop in different ways. Lyuka cannot wait to grow up. She is still an "ugly duckling," though already with traits of the beauty of a future swan.

Liza is more complex; the graceful blond, grey-eyed, girl makes heads turn. When she is with the admirer Cromwell, she wants to be treated as an adult. But to Andrei, her brother's pal, she confesses: "I keep thinking that living must be abominable, if it's true that childhood is the best part of life. Since later it's going to be worse, I don't want to grow up. And you know, I think that I won't, ever..."

Though both Lyuka and Liza have only vague memories of Russia, for Lyuka it is the splendid image of Petrograd and the Neva in winter, and her childish infatuation with the dark-eyed elf on the blue ice. For Liza it is Moscow "invaded by tigers, military ships, parrots from her father's voyages, from his stories." Being familiar with the poverty of émigré life, both girls "respect wealth." Yet Lyuka rejoices like a child about gifts received from her sister, who is married to a well-to-do man. She herself lives on dreams about the imaginary love of her "elf" Arseniy and once angrily rebukes her friend's cousin, who dared to touch her knee.

As for Liza, in spite of being fond of Andrei, she derives pleasure from kissing Cromwell and permits him to spend money not only on her but also on her brother and his friends. Lyuka behaves seductively with Arseniy. Liza is even more sexually open; she is ready to make young men happy -- Andrei out of love, Cromwell out of gratitude, and her cousin Leslie because he later takes care of her. Nevertheless, one is under the impression that Odoevtseva tries to protect her young heroines from premature physical intimacy: her male characters almost always refrain from taking advantage of the girls' youth and inexperience. It is frightening to imagine how easily an unscrupulous man could seize the opportunity to victimize them, especially "motherless" Liza with her fearless trustfulness and desire to be liked. The author, who does not in any case go into physical detail, does not specify that Liza's relationship remains platonic; readers can only guess. Yet they are reassured in the final scene of the novel, when Liza says that she "never, never... with no one..." and that Andrei is the only one. One cannot help but believe her simple confession: "I'm happy that it is today. With you."

Andrei leaves a mixed impression upon the reader. His friendship with Kolya, an irresponsible gambler and cynic, does not speak in his favour. But he is in love with Liza, Kolya's sister. He has no parents and lives at his aunt's. All this makes it easy for Kolya to dominate Andrei and even to make him an accomplice in a horrible crime. Andrei is a weakling but finds enough courage to commit suicide in the picnic house where they murdered Cromwell. He is overjoyed that Liza has returned to the house on the same day: "You know, I kept thinking about you all these days and called you. I'm so glad you didn't come too late... and I'm still here."

Andrei insists on Liza's going back to her cousin in Normandy but begs her to remain with him till her last train is due at ten-thirty at night. She decides not to think about anything sad and terrible:

"Liza, I've always loved no one but you... and was very jealous... because of the other," he adds almost in a whisper.

Later, Andrei talks excitedly of Liza's future, not suspecting that she has decided to die with him: "Liza, you could have a baby... just think of it -- our baby, yours and mine,"' he whispers hurriedly. "Promise me not to do anything. Let it be born. You will look into its eyes and remember me. Our baby."

Odoevtseva describes Kolya quite differently. He disdainfully speaks in the morning about Odette, Lisa's friend, with whom he has spent the night: "She won't let me go... I'm sick and tired of her." But later in the evening, necking with Odette on the rear seat of Cromwell's automobile, he completely ignores Liza's and Cromwell's presence. He talks mockingly of his mother: "Now she is fighting with Krolik, and later she'll either get hysterical or leave for the dressmaker's."

Kolya worries only about how to get more money to pay for his pleasures. The fifty francs allowance from his mother is nothing at all in his opinion. On learning that a wealthy Englishman is in love with Liza, he begins to use her as bait. After they are refused admittance to a casino because of Liza's age, he cuts her long curls while she sleeps to make her look older. Envious of the wealthy Cromwell, Kolya abandons all conscience and pride and makes the former pay all the bills at casinos and restaurants. And when Cromwell's money is exhausted and even his car is pawned, Kolya furiously exclaims: "Damned

Crom! No money. But he himself told me that his mother keeps her money in an unlocked safe and doesn't even know how many diamonds she owns."

Obviously, Kolya finds it natural to take advantage of Cromwell's mother's trustfulness. Realizing that Cromwell could not be persuaded just to steal the money, Kolya invents a perfidious plan: he and Andrei supposedly belong to a monarchist organization, which has entrusted them with an important secret assignment in Soviet Russia. He promises to take Cromwell and Liza with him, if the former will bring his mother's valuables "for the cause" ("the end justifies the means") It proves very easy to convince Liza, with her love for Russia. The romantic Cromwell is ready for any sacrifice for the sake of his Isolde.

Kolya orders Liza to invite Cromwell for the farewell night before their "departure", thus arousing Andrei's jealousy and hatred toward the Englishman and making him a willing accomplice in the crime.

Having obtained the valuables from Cromwell, Kolya orders him to write a letter to his mother telling her he will be absent for three months, and explaining why he took the money and the valuables (apparently hoping thus to divert the search from Paris). To finish off Cromwell and burn his belongings without being disturbed, Kolya sends Liza away from the house and then tells her that the trip has been canceled because Cromwell changed his mind, decided not to go, and left the house. The money and valuables have now been returned to him.

It would seem that in Kolya we are faced with a cruel, ruthless criminal. But the author also shows him to us in moments of human weakness -- pale and suffering from insomnia and fear. Here we see him after doing away with Cromwell and coming into Liza's room with a "guilty and confused smile": "Lizochka, I woke you up, please forgive me... Andrei and I can't get to sleep. Our nerves are on edge with this trip, with this whole business... Come to our room, Lizochka. Stay with us for a while and chat with us... Tomorrow we'll buy you a fox-collar..." His tone alternates between plaintive and ingratiating.

Most readers would be struck by the promise of a fox collar. If the money and valuables had been returned to Cromwell, where did Kolya get the money for a fox collar? But Liza is shaken by the words that they are not going to Russia and hardly notices the contradiction. The Englishman Cromwell is characterized by Odoevtseva with obvious sympathy, which the reader shares from the very first page: "It was on such an ocean that Isolde sailed to meet Tristan." The youth reminisces about the Scottish meadows, the castle with sumptuous rooms, Eton, et cetera. Life in Biarritz seems to him crazy, gay, and immoral with its "irritating atmosphere, silly books, and constant expectation, everlasting premonition of love."

Cromwell has also lost one parent, his father having been killed in the war. His mother loves him in her own way; she is proud of him but does not know how to be affectionate. Having fallen in love with Liza, Cromwell also treats her brother and friends with kindness and pays for all their entertainment. He is open and honest and does not think it possible to encounter baseness and falsehood in others.

Here he is in a restaurant, pouring champagne for everybody: "We must drink to our friendship", he says, "but to a true one... to a friendship forever, for life and death."

Lisa laughingly raises her glass: "I drink only to life", she says, "but to the whole life."

Cromwell then hands Kolya a glass: "In that case", he says, "you and I will drink to death."

At the age of only sixteen, Cromwell believes in love and friendship. It seems to him that he has found what he was searching for. This explains the naïveté that makes him believe Kolya and agree to something which he would normally find unthinkable.

Here is his exchange with Liza before their "departure to Russia":

"Tomorrow night you will have the diamonds."

"Crom, you are an angel."

He shook his head sadly: "Angels don't steal."

"You find it very hard to do that?"

"Terribly hard," he said seriously. "To die would be easier."

"Is it possible that to steal should be harder than to die?"

Cromwell lowered his head.

"Infinitely so."

Liza looked at him curiously. "I don't understand. I am afraid of death."

But Liza does not forget this conversation. Vague suspicions and premonitions keep tormenting her. The next day, when Cromwell brings the money and jewellery, she begs him to forget about the trip to Russia and to return the valuables before his mother wakes.

"It is too late anyway. I'm a thief. You are the only reason for me to carry on living."

"I'm so grateful to you that I would not refuse you any of your wishes." He moved away from her, even slightly pushing her away. "Not that... I'm happy as it is... But when we return from Russia, as grownups, we'll get married." He embraced her again.

The impression made on the reader by the touching scenes Odoevtseva depicts is especially strong on second reading, when knowledge of the ending reveals the hidden, deeper meaning of Liza's and Cromwell's conversation.

Neither Kolya nor Andrei, in his jealous torment, would have believed that Cromwell feels not only love but also tenderness and compassion for this young girl who is still hardly more than a child. He assumes responsibility for her and is glad to be able to protect her.

As for Liza, her gratitude to Cromwell is mixed with a motherly compassion. One day they lie together, fully dressed on a wide sofa. Watching him asleep, she straightens the blanket under his chin, and thinks: "Just like a little boy. As though he were my son..." This is a quite different Liza from the carefree, aggressive girl we met on the beach in Biarritz at the beginning of the novel.

Liza is much more difficult to analyze from fragments of phrases, hints, ellipses and inferences than the other characters of the novel. Though heredity no doubt plays an important role in shaping character, one should not underestimate the influence of childhood environment and especially the relationship with one's mother. What, then, are Liza's feelings for the still beautiful, elegantly dressed woman, who allows herself to be called "mother" only on rare occasions when no one else is around? (Kolya and Liza must pose as orphans, being raised by their "cousine" Natasha. Though only a few of their acquaintances believe this version, she strictly insists that her children stick to it.)

Here, Liza meets Rokhlin Krolik, who is waiting at the house for Natasha's return. He is always outspoken with Liza, who sympathizes with him and silently listens to his accusations against her mother: "She's shameless... cruel, mean... Now she tortures me... Now she is there with her lover Boris..."

Though Liza knows she should be insulted on her mother's behalf, she feels sorry and tries to console Krolik, who is so unhappy while Natasha basks in admiration.

In another scene Liza watches Natasha on a train from Biarritz to Paris. Boris has not kept his promise to join them, and Natasha is pale and upset. Looking at her mother, Liza thinks: "She doesn't look that beautiful. I look better." And she is glad to have the opportunity for a first class trip.

Later, Natasha's red and swollen eyes, her complaints about migraine and sleepless nights make Liza conclude: "When a lover deceives you, one calls it migraine. I must tell that to Kolya."

Nevertheless, Liza often thinks about her mother's fate. Even while enjoying herself in a restaurant and listening to jazz, she has a vision of Natasha crying, then singing the Russian song "Black Eyes".

On another occasion we find Liza on a rainy day, shedding tears as she reads a Dostoyevsky novel: "Oh, God, this is so beautiful, how ignorant I was before..."

Liza feels that she has grown up and cries out of pity, admiration and goodness. Her thoughts get confused: "one must do something... not for oneself, but for others. Sacrifice oneself, perish..."
She awaits her mother's return to pour out all her love and tenderness. One should not blame her, poor soul, she thinks, one has to pity and love her. Liza decides to make her mother happy. Unfortunately, she gets no chance to talk to her mother. In the morning Boris is there. Liza hears his voice, which she suddenly begins to hate: "Yes, that turned out to be a smart move... One will never get lost with you." Boris is exulting over the money Natasha has wangled from Rokhlin. Full of joy, her mother leaves for Nice that same evening.

Later, Liza consoles the betrayed victim Krolik: "She has abandoned me also and I'm very unhappy..." Then, alone again, she sighs: "Poor Krolik... poor mother, we're all unhappy. And none of us understand the other... How difficult, how terrible life is."

Though she never gets the chance to talk to her mother, Liza decides to write her a long letter, telling her that she loves her more than anything in the world and would devote her life to her. Then a postcard arrives describing life in Nice as gay and wonderful. But when Liza sees the words "For God's sake don't forget to call me 'Natasha' " scribbled across the sky and the sea, she tears up her letter to her mother and never thinks of her again.

Only on the day when Liza is preparing to die with Andrei does she find in the house another letter from Nice: "I lost my money gambling and they wouldn't let me leave the hotel... If you are short of cash, Kolya should speak to Krolik..." Here Liza stops reading the letter. Her feelings toward her mother have now run the full gamut, from sarcastic criticism through an outburst of love, tenderness and compassion, to complete indifference.

All the greater therefore is Liza's need for love, which she seeks outside her family. Thus, at age twelve she falls in love with Andrei, her brother's friend. At fourteen, after being separated from Andrei, she enjoys Cromwell's attention and infatuation. She even gets attached to him and is saddened at leaving Biarritz, although he promises to come to Paris in two weeks. In the train she thinks of him, admires his bouquet of roses and feels sorry for him. But the approaching meeting with Andrei begins to chase away thoughts of Cromwell, and when she leaves the train, she decides not to take the roses with her and pushes them aside with her foot.

Two weeks later in Paris, when Cromwell repeats that he loves her, she sighs sadly: "Oh, who needs this? Don't say it any more." Still, she does not reject his invitation to go to a restaurant to enjoy themselves. She becomes animated and dances repeatedly with both Cromwell and Andrei.

But when the gaiety stops -- Cromwell is out of money -- Liza coolly sends him home. "It's disgusting," she says to her girl-friend.

Liza now thinks more often of Andrei. She is tormented by his coldness and indifference: "Could this be love? Is it worth living if this is love?"

The reader might conclude that Liza is interested only in having a good time and that she is striving to love because of the awakening of the woman in her. But Liza knows of another kind of love, about which she never speaks to anybody. Thus, after Cromwell's "bankruptcy" on a rainy, cheerless Christmas Eve without presents or even a Christmas tree, she is alone and her thoughts fly again to Russia. She remembers Christmas in Moscow: light, sparkling snow, sleighs driven by beautiful horses. As a child she had often asked her mother to tell her about Moscow, but always got the same reply: "Leave me alone... When you get to Moscow, you'll see for yourself."

When Liza was nine years old, she had overheard a conversation between her nanny and the house-maid Dasha: "It's for our sins. For our sins. There is our mistress. She came here, left Russia and forgot about it. Now she runs around in theatres and restaurants and waits for somebody to return Russia to her. No, no nonsense, one has to suffer for Russia. Suffer." Now Liza recollects her meticulously planned escape on a steamer going to Russia. She planned to hide herself in the hold, just like a boy in a book she had read. She had foreseen everything. Nuts, figs, chocolate and the 14 francs and 30 centimes she had saved up, all tied up in a handkerchief, seemed to her to be all the supplies she would need to get her to Le Havre. She left at daybreak and managed to get away. But the milkwoman, who had heard about her disappearance, recognized her and brought her back: "Imagine! She covered ten kilometres! Such a little girl!"

On recollecting the details of her return home, Liza relives her shame. She had told her mother, sobbing, that she was going to the boat that was going to Russia in order to suffer. She thought she would never survive her disgrace when she heard loud laughter from the next room. Since then, Liza decided to think about Russia only when she was alone, like now on this Christmas Eve in Paris.

But these thoughts show the reader a different Liza and it becomes clear that she would accept Kolya's plan like a Christmas miracle. "To Russia... Is it true? I'll die of happiness... I'll do everything, everything..."

There reawakens in Liza the little girl of Trouville who tried to run away on a steamer to Russia in order to suffer. She sees an angel in her dreams and believes she is destined for some great feat like Joan of Arc. "This is happiness... She needed nothing, neither Andrei nor love."

Cromwell is puzzled by the change in Liza.

"Has some misfortune befallen you, Isolde?" -- "Misfortune? No, a great joy awaits me. See, we're going to Russia. I've never been so happy."

Cromwell cannot be indifferent to Liza's excitement. He also is carried away by the noble purpose of going to Russia and promises his help. And, of course, he agrees to go along. Liza is now convinced that her wish will be fulfilled.

Odoevtseva paints the portrait of Isolde with such love that readers are ready to believe that Liza is the victim of a cruel deception. With the perfidy of a Iago, her brother finds an answer to each of her questions, dispelling the slightest shadow of doubt. When he fires the house-maid Dasha, Liza approves: nobody is supposed to know about their departure. Then she hears, from behind the door: "Shoot him in the back. Wrap up the barrel of the gun." When she asks Kolya about it, he replies: "Who knows whom I will have to shoot... a border guard or a chekist. Why do you think I'm going to Russia, to catch butterflies?" And, although faint suspicions darken her faith several times, Liza still believes.

There can certainly be no doubt of Kolya's and Andrei's guilt. They are motivated not by hunger or survival but by envy, jealousy and hatred.

It is harder for the reader to judge Liza. She believed because she wanted to believe, and she dismissed all doubts because she feared the destruction of her faith in the fulfillment of her long-standing desire to go to Russia.

When Kolya tells her that Cromwell has quarreled with them and left, taking the money and diamonds with him, she is shaken. She only remembers the words "We're not going," and can think of nothing else. Could she possibly believe Cromwell had left through the back door while she obeyed Kolya's instructions, guarding the front of the house in order not to let anybody in? "Don't think, don't think", she keeps on telling herself. And when she hears from the bathroom a horrible sound as though someone were scraping the floor with a brush, she decides it is of no concern to her. She lies down and counts to a hundred, endeavouring to fall asleep.

How much of the truth does she guess in the morning when she sees Kolya and Andrei leaving with two heavily packed suitcases? Excited and full of fear, she decides to run away and never return to this house.

Later, surrounded by the tender care of her cousin Leslie in his hunting lodge in Normandy, Liza has apparently forgotten her past life, Andrei, her brother, Paris... "She never thought

'that thing' through to the end; she never understood what had happened. Perhaps nothing had happened."
      Is it possible? The reader wonders. And the author instantly gives the answer.
      One evening Liza suddenly "sees" Cromwell with a copper candlestick in his hand. He smiles, trying to tell her something but leaves silently. Memories assail her like a whirlwind: the scraping of the brush in the bathroom, the suitcases -- how could she possibly not remember? She decides to leave for Paris that same evening, not knowing why. She is tormented as she realizes her guilt. Hasn't she been only pretending that she knows and remembers nothing?
      In the pink house she finds Andrei, her Tristan.
      When one tries to penetrate the innermost recesses of the characters in this novel, one reluctantly finds that they all have something in common. And one remembers a passage from one of Odoevtseva's poems:

"... My loneliness, your loneliness,
ours, yours, their loneliness".

      Almost all Odoevtseva's heroes are marked with the stamp of loneliness.
      The mother Natasha is lonely and unhappy in spite of her steady stream of admirers. Cromwell, who never shares his thoughts about his friends, not even with his mother, is lonely too. Andrei is also lonely; though in love with Liza, he is unhappy, and has shrunk into himself with his jealousy of Cromwell. And, of course, Liza/Isolde is no less lonely, alongside her brother, whom she fears and does not respect. She is in love with Andrei and suffers from his coolness. They are all wounded by love, obsession, passion -- though some feel pain, and others think themselves happy.
      Perhaps it is because these characters are so sick with the incurable disease called life, that they lose their conscience, pride and dignity. They will tolerate and forgive insults, humiliation and betrayal. Natasha confides to her girlfriend that Boris

even hits her: "But can I forget him?.. With or without him it is the end for me." At the same time, she plays the same kind of undignified game with Rokhlin, the man who is ready to die for her in spite of her unfaithfulness.

Krolik is the only survivor. He comes to realize that life is still possible even without the woman who exerted an evil power over him.

"This was the end. She's left me... like a mangy dog. At that moment he realized that this was really the end. But not the end that he had awaited and feared. No, it was the end of his slavery, the end of his love... The end of his ruination... His step became light, he breathed more easily, the trees rumoured softly, and in the sky the moon sailed lightly through black clouds."

In the fate of all the other heroes we find a steady deepening of tragic shadow. Even the title of the novel suggests that Liza's life will have no happy fulfillment. Premonitions of tragedy torture her even as she prepares for the long-awaited trip to Russia. On the eve of that day she says to her brother: "Kolya, I am scared today. As though from every corner..." Later she tries to talk Cromwell out of the trip, without really knowing why. She feels that he is exposed to danger, and when Cromwell asks her why she is crying, she answers: "Because we have so little of life left."

A similar premonition forces Cromwell's usually cold-blooded mother to wake up in a state of strange confusion. "An animal-like fear for her son rapidly ran through her body and rose to her throat..." And as Cromwell comes to Liza's home for the first time, he suddenly stops and has to fight down a premonition that unhappiness awaits him in this house. Waiting in the hall, he sees on the table one glove, which resembles a cut-off hand: "the empty fingers sadly faced upwards, as though chasing away or cursing..."

Odoevtseva's teacher Gumilyov used to teach the young poets that a day without a poem was a lost day. Why then did Odoevtseva, the pride of his studio, turn exclusively to novels within a few years of his death? One could attribute this shift to the conditions of émigré life, to her husband's advice and to practical considerations. She soon realized that there were in fact more poets than actual readers of poetry. But many émigré poets remained only poets and neither sought other means of expression nor possessed the ability to work in a different genre. There must have been other reasons for Odoevtseva's attraction to the novel.

It is not uncommon for poets, in their maturity, to feel constrained by the framework of lyrical poetry and to turn to other forms. But Odoevtseva was unusual in that she sought early on to escape that framework, creating a contemporary ballad at the very beginning of her career. She surprised literary St. Petersburg with her precocious daring and almost mystical penetration into the human soul. Less than ten years after fame first touched her "still adolescent brow", Western critics were praising her first novel for its insight into the human heart. Nevertheless, Odoevtseva's "prose" suggests that she never ceased to view the world with the eyes of a poet. Her precise, simple language is constantly penetrated by poetry that makes one line sparkle or illuminates whole pages. Indeed, the most common things can become poetry.

For example, a pair of discarded silk stockings "lie there as two small warm lumps, just like recently shot birds." And Liza's locks, cut off at night by her brother, lie spread on the pillow "like shiny, live snakes curled up in a ring in the sunshine."

Odoevtseva also remains a poet when contemplating nature: "A shredded white cloud flowed slowly in the dark and empty sky."

The tone of her story-telling is lively and, at the same time, quietly controlled. She avoids exclamation marks, even in phrases and words that express worry or fear. Thus, in the scene of the escape from the pink house: "her heart did not beat, but only murmured imperceptibly. Run, run. If you fall, you're lost."

Odoevtseva never moralizes, not even through the heroes' thoughts and words, about the crime or the lowering of morals. Actions themselves bear witness to the malaise of these half-grown people. Each reader can evaluate the conversation and thoughts of the novel's characters. The author does not consider Isolde either good or bad, but uses an endless variety and combination of colours to paint her portrait. We usually look for prototypes in novels and poems. One remembers Bunin's comment that no matter how an author tries to hide behind the back of his heroes, they inevitably give him away. The book -- is his author! Flaubert put it even more bluntly: "Madame Bovary -- that's me."

Whether intentionally or not, Odoevtseva gives Liza/ Isolde some traits of her own youth, as shown in her memoirs. Of her love of Russia, especially St. Petersburg, we read relatively little in *On the Banks of the Neva*. She hides it in her soul and we often only guess her secret. But the many pages devoted to Liza's exultation at the possibility of seeing Russia again are so full of fire that readers cannot help but hear the author's voice, feel the depth and strength of Odoevtseva's love for her native land.

Here is Liza already counting the hours till the time when they leave.

"In this motionless, slow life everything was happy, passionate expectation. It seemed to Liza that her heart, set on fire on Christmas Eve by Kolya's words 'Do you want to go to Russia?' was still burning in her breast. She was surprised that it did not burn even more strongly and utterly consume her."

It is impossible to quote here even the most poetic lines where Liza, as a nine-year-old girl or as an adolescent, speaks of her selfless love for Russia. Here the author's terse self-control gives way to the sweep of the artist's brush.

But in the touching scene in the rose house, when Lisa and Andrei fulfill at long last their unspoken desire, the author returns to her style of compact description and terse dialogue laden with emotion. In contrast to present-day writers and cinematographers, who shamelessly penetrate bedrooms for lingering erotic close-ups, Odoevtseva noiselessly draws the curtain, protecting her lovers from curious eyes.

Andrei does not know of Liza's decision to die with him. He is sure she will listen to his advice and will return to

Leslie on the last night train. "Liza, Liza, don't fall asleep... We have only two hours left..." But then he himself falls asleep. Liza, half asleep, feels pain, weakness and tiredness, "as though she had been run over by a street-car". She knows that she must leave immediately, but not go away for good. Out in the street, by their fence stands a man with a moustache, a man who is wearing a black top hat. He saw her enter the house. Andrei is unaware, however -- let him sleep.

We see Liza at the gas range. Turn on the gas jet... so simple. Then, lying down next to Andrei who embraces her without awakening, she shuts her eyes with pleasure: "now nothing of this hostile, terrifying, foreign world can cause them any harm."

And without thinking of the degree of their guilt, readers close the book with a feeling of compassion for the fate of these half-children who part with this life without having learned its main values -- half-children not stoical enough to survive the wounds inflicted on their souls in the past, where one should really look for the beginning of their end.

* * *

The Mirror ("Zerkalo")

In her two previous novels, *Angel of Death* and *Isolde* Irina Odoevtseva shows courage in her choice of plot. In *The Mirror*, on the other hand, she sensitively describes the eternal human emotions of love, tenderness, passion, happiness, grief, and loneliness.

The heroine, Lyuka, whom we know from the novel *Angel of Death* is now a twenty-year-old married woman. The author devotes the most poetic pages of the book to Lyuka's inner drama, leaving the other characters in the shadow. Yet they are nonetheless memorable for their sometimes contradictory traits.

This novel was published in 1939, twelve years after the appearance of the *Angel of Death*. Almost the whole edition was sold to Germans in occupied France. It is unknown how many copies were bought by Russian emigrants.

The Mirror, at first sight, could pass for a novel with love as a leitmotif; but war was not the right time for such a novel. Today, more than fifty years later, this novel is naturally, almost unknown to Russian readers; even those who had read it at that time could not remember details. Therefore, I shall briefly describe the plot before analyzing the novel's characters.

The very famous film director Thiery Rivoir "discovers" Lyuka by chance. He offers her the principal role in his new film and promises her stardom.

She soon realizes that she loves him: not in the fanciful, imaginary way she had loved a man in her adolescent years (described in *The Angel of Death*) but truly and passionately. On Rivoir's insistence she moves into his house, leaving Pavel Dal, her loving husband. Gradually, Rivoir gets more and more attracted to her and is even ready to marry her. But when he learns that, while still in her teens, she had involuntarily caused the death of her sister, who curses Lyuka on her deathbed, he superstitiously fears she will bring him bad luck and leaves her, even though he knows she is pregnant.

At some moments of merciless self-flagellation Lyuka concludes that "... there is nothing unusually tragic or unique either in her love or in her grief. It is all commonplace. Hundreds of women live through the same."

Nevertheless, the author devotes the book to Lyuka's love, happiness and grief. Why? After the sensational success of the novel *Angel of Death,* especially its English translation, some critics and friends (and even her husband, the poet Georgi Ivanov) had mistakenly concluded that Odoevtseva was at her best when penetrating the psychology of a young teenage girl.

This prompted Odoevtseva to choose another young girl as the heroine of her next novel, *Isolde.* But then, as though wishing to prove that she was capable of describing the scale of emotions of a still young but married woman, she created *The Mirror.* As always, the decisive factor was not so much the plot but the insight into the mind and soul of her heroine.

As if to prove her critics doubly wrong, she portrays a Lyuka, five years older than in *The Angel of Death* and changed to such a degree that readers can hardly recognize her.

As in her previous novels, the author characterizes the heroine only gradually. We learn about the changes in her looks from other characters' remarks, scattered through the pages of the book. The image we build from those remarks again reminds us of Odoevtseva's own portrait in her youth.

We remember Lyuka the teenager. Though not unattractive, she was considered an "ugly duckling" compared to her beautiful older sister Vera. Now... but let us hear how the other characters of the novel describe her...

Here's how Rivoir sees her: "Your face is young, entirely new, as if straight from the shelf of a store; still not creased or soiled by life and memories... touching, somehow impossible to look at without tears... you never disappoint one... always as needed at the given moment... with no need for correction or change."

Rivoir's partner Guéraint, too, sees her as close to perfection: "...you always seem to be lit by a projector... always in a circle of light... no matter how many people surround you..."

Even his daughter Laurence thinks of her as "the most admirable woman in the world... wearing an ermine coat, she resembles a snow maiden."

A Soviet tourist whom she meets on a train concludes, looking at her eyes reddened by tears: "You can even afford to cry because everything enhances you. You are so beautiful that it even seems supernatural..."

Pavel Dal, her former husband, recollects: "...she would walk on the street, swiftly and lightly, as if rushing to an encounter with joy... She'd turn each day into a holiday..."

Odoevtseva's contemporaries and the readers of her memoirs may find great similarities between the author and this portrait of Lyuka.

As for Lyuka's inner life, the author of *The Mirror* reveals it only through the thoughts and reflections of her heroine. And the changes in the teenager from *The Angel of Death* are startling. Lyuka is no longer a bold, lively, happy girl, witty, at times aggressive and demanding. Apparently the Gypsy's song was prophetic:

> There has been grief,
> There will be grief,
> Grief will never end.

What, then, has happened to Lyuka since we parted with her in the days of her first dark grief?

The events in *The Mirror* occur almost chronologically, interrupted rarely by flashbacks. We meet Lyuka, the wife of Pavel Dal, a modest, kind and loving husband, the day after her long awaited miracle: she has been "discovered," during a festival, by Thiery Rivoir himself. This morning is for her not only the dawn of a new day: she now feels, believes, "knows -- although very vaguely -- that 'yesterday' will move into the distant past. Yet today she still remembers even the smallest details of the fateful last evening."

At the festival attended by the select society of Paris, the country's president himself is present. She sees herself as poorly attired despite many hours spent dressing in her very best. She muses, gazing at Rivoir's visiting card, which would open the door for her into a world that, till now, was inaccessible.

Even the very first pages of the novel do not provide a black-and-white photograph of events. Rather, they present a sequence of poems in which we discover new colours, nuances and metaphors at every rereading. It is impossible to select the most striking and original ones; each line is a new spark, each paragraph -- a new poem. We soon conclude that *The Mirror* is not a novel: it is a collection of rare poetic verses disguised as long, straight lines of "prose". The reader who can discern them under their mask would see them joyfully leap from the page with such intensity that, blinded for a moment, he would close his eyes to savour this delight.

The lines interflow, turning into melody, they sing about Lyuka's feelings of humiliation and envy; poor Lyuka, alone amidst this festive display of wealth and luxury. She is tortured by a singer's voice that "painfully reverberates in all of her body, drilling her bones like rheumatism, like old age..." Promising hope, the voice rises higher and higher, growing more enticing "...yet submits to the sobering voice of the piano and falls head over heels... Lyuka's last hope is crushed at her feet in the thunder of chords."

She hears in the voice of the singer the story of her unsuccessful life, of her cruel fate. It hits her as a sudden revelation without warning or preparation, "not gradually as... when misfortune opens, like a flower: at first bloom... soft silky leaves... pale green bud... hesitantly, very slowly, an accumulation of fears and doubts; when there's enough time to get accustomed to the misguided fate, so that when the flower fully opens in all its final magnificence you aren't frightened and obediently accept each... petal".

For Lyuka the voice of the singer brutally and mercilessly reveals her fate; "her pain, suppressed, rolled down her cheek as a tear... diminishing her grief by one drop." This very tear on her cheek, noted by Rivoir, marks the beginning of a new chapter in Lyuka's life, a chapter about her fame, great happiness, and deep sorrow -- all that is reflected in this book's prose, set to the music of poetry.

The reader may wonder just who is this Thiery Rivoir who has inspired the heroine (and the author) to so many poetic lines, almost songs?

To Lyuka he seems like an archangel who descended from heaven in light and glory. His smile was "like the sparkling of candelabras in the palace of Versailles, like thousands of burning candles in a cathedral... like the reflection of Northern lights in transparent ice..."

But all this happened yesterday. Today she is sitting next to him in an automobile, and the trees of the Bois de Boulogne are swiftly passing by. He is happy with his "discovery". The fact that she is married disappoints him, but not for long, since to his question whether she loves her husband, Lyuka quickly answers: "No, not at all." He is not surprised; to him, a husband is an "unnecessary burden".

He speaks enthusiastically about his new film and his plan to make her famous. When talking about women, he mentions Theresa Kassani, his aged "discovery." "...Women can never understand... they are tactless and jealous. Why do they so easily fall in love, without being able to fall out of it? Each wants to be the only one. With each it must be forever..."

He does not remember any of them. His life is marked by an abundance of energy, by ambition, struggle, and victory.

He has a sharp eye and those who start with him always "climb the ladder of fame." He is so used to conquest that he invites Lyuka to his place the very day her husband leaves on a business trip. Her rejection spurs him to resolve: next time! After their first night together, while driving her home, he suddenly starts whistling "loudly and diligently with obvious pleasure, the tune of a march with ringing trills... merrily, triumphantly... 'Don't I whistle well? Eh?'" The next day she signs a contract with him.

We see Rivoir through Lyuka's eyes and hear his voice during rare moments of their conversations. Her infatuation makes her admire all his actions. "...He smiles his electric smile, it is so dazzling; it radiates wealth, power, and glory."

Infatuation does not prevent her from seeing his weaknesses. She cannot justify them, yet does not judge him harshly.

But the reader remembers them; the result, in my opinion, is that Rivoir cannot evoke even simple respect as a human being.

He, for instance, doesn't care that Lyuka is used to a warm, dark bedroom, and keeps the windows wide open all through the night. While making the film and dictating his will in every detail, he often kills her self-confidence with cutting remarks: "...I've made a mistake... you have no talent... but nevertheless, I will make you famous."

We see him as a shallow, egoistic, self-enamoured person despite his ability and success. He has never finished a book, has never listened to an opera, yet would talk about everything like a connoisseur.

Only once, perhaps, has he talked sincerely -- at Lyuka's request -- about his childhood. His father was a barber, handsome and good-natured, with a comb behind his ear. Thiery used to be ashamed of him and, in fact, hated his father so intensely that he felt he could even kill him. He would have preferred to be a son of a murderer or a hangman. He despised his mother for being a slave to his father.

At sixteen he left for Paris and never went back. He reveals to Lyuka that he is afraid of driving and considers her his protection against death. Much later he shows cruel cowardice by making Lyuka tell him the truth about her sister's death. It horrifies him to learn that Vera, before dying, had cursed Lyuka. Although agreeing that Lyuka was innocent, he no longer believes that she will bring him good luck. His love for her, the desire to marry her and have a son with her -- all is forgotten: "I will go bankrupt... I'm afraid of you... you're as repulsive to me as a toad... I hate you."

When his premonitions prove to be false and the film starring Lyuka brings him new wealth and fame, he takes his own life. Yet, even this step could hardly have been motivated by repentance. Rather, it may have been the fear that Lyuka's death had not been an accident but suicide, and that his own guilt will sooner or later cause his downfall.

Here, too, Odoevtseva avoids naturalistic description of his death and leaves it to the reader to guess the real cause of Rivoir's suicide. The only detail that leads to the possibility of repentance is a piece of paper with the words apparently scribbled on subconsciously: "...next to Lyudmila Dal."

Only at the very end of the book one of the personages remarks in passing: "Today is exactly a month since Thiery Rivoir shot himself." This was the man with whom Lyuka had known the heaven of happiness and the abyss of despair and who had become her only *raison d'être*. Was he really worthy of such devotion and self-sacrifice?

The famous Russian literary critic Belinsky, in his analysis of the Lisa - Chatsky - Molchalin* triangle, concluded: "One could judge a woman's value by knowing the man she loves." Wouldn't this theory answer the reader's question about Lyuka's love for Rivoir? Are they not both egoistic and egocentric?

She considered her husband's love a burden ("What for? Who needs it?"). Rivoir later thought the same about her love for him.

In the studio, where Rivoir is disliked, Lyuka is considered odious. She finds out about this only later, in Venice, when

---

* Griboyedov: "Woe from Wit"

Rivoir has abandoned her. Before, she cared only about herself and her happiness with him without even noticing her colleagues, without thinking that they might need help, or at least compassion. Rivoir, as described by the author, reads nothing but newspapers. But Lyuka, too, is never seen reading a book. It might be argued that, during film-making, a star who is also in love with her director would have neither time nor strength for reading after an exhausting day in the studio. But even as Pavel Dal's stay-at-home wife, she had never visited a library and would sit, bored, at an open window -- "sit there, with no desire to do anything, yet feeling, through her boredom, the gradual accumulation of life's energy within her..." Much later, admitting her ignorance of literature during a conversation with a Soviet tourist, she remarks that all she knew about Chekhov's *Three Sisters* was that they dreamed of moving to Moscow; she had never read the whole play.

While depressed at times by the drabness of life on husband Pavel's modest means, she had never tried to contribute to their income. On the other hand, her "heartless" sister Vera (*Angel of Death*) used to help their mother by doing needlework for a store.

Lyuka renounces her husband during her first meeting with Rivoir ("...I don't love him at all.") While moving out, she tries to suppress pity for him: "There is no other way... in comparison with Thiery, Pavel simply doesn't exist."

Only after her death do we learn, from Pavel's reminiscences, about the circumstances of their marriage. He had met her at the home of mutual acquaintances and fell in love immediately... because of her laughter. There was something fatherly in his love for her. As for her, marriage was like the beginning of another childhood. He even presented her with a teddy bear as a wedding gift. "What I love most is to feed you, bathe you and put you to sleep. I would prefer to have you not as a wife, but as a daughter..."

On hearing that she had signed a contract with Rivoir without consulting him, Pavel said: "I always thought that your fate, Lyuka, would be a very special one... but this is too unexpected."

Odoevtseva does not devote many lines to Pavel. We learn only after her death that "when she abandoned him, he often thought of ways to end his life." We also learn that she had met him -- only once -- in a café and said guiltily: "Don't die, Pavel, please, I might still need you in the future."

He lives on with that hope, despite the torments of love, jealousy, hurt, and even desire for revenge. And he actually did have a chance to be "useful" to her, though not in the way he had expected.

It is he who, albeit unwittingly, helps to create the legend of Lyudmila Dal the film star, by sharing memories of her with Laurence Guéraint, the daughter of Rivoir's partner. Laurence eagerly asks Pavel about the childhood, tastes, and habits of the beloved actress.

The Lyuka Pavel describes is absolutely pure and white: "She was a girl in a white dress, the way she looked in her coffin."

Pavel's idealized reminiscences evoke in Laurence the desire to put on Lyuka's grave a monument in the shape of an angel (her role in Rivoir's film), a wish fulfilled by Laurence's father, Guéraint.

The author -- quite in Lyuka's spirit -- arranges a future for this romantic, dreamy Laurence with Pavel, as if to make up to him for the suffering Lyuka caused him.

More than one page of the book is lovingly devoted to the exalted young Laurence. She had grown up without her mother, educated by rival governesses. Her father had always been cool and reserved towards her, "such a strange, successful, self-satisfied person."

She could not love him, and therefore felt guilty about him -- and not only about him. She was tormented by a "vague feeling of responsibility for everything -- for the beggar on the street corner, for a train collision, for a dog killed by a stranger's automobile..."

Even as a child she used to resent the abundance of expensive toys, and in private school she suffered from the girls' envious remarks about her father's wealth, remarks that suggested it was unnecessary for her study hard, since she would never have to work for a living anyway.

The reader cannot help but notice the contrast between Lyuka and Laurence. The former, embarrassed by her early poverty, later easily gets accustomed to an automobile, brocade, velvet, and silver foxes. Laurence, the heiress, used to dream of sharing a small apartment with her father and helping him in the office. She was ashamed of her father's large house and racehorse stables; she even dislikes being called pretty.

Lyuka, on the other hand, accepts her sudden wealth as a worthy ornament for her beauty. We never find her contemplating evil: Laurence's *weltschmerz* is foreign to her nature.

Although she never tries to change anything, Laurence at least is aware of the existence of "homeless people freezing under bridges... starving children and kittens drowned in a pail..."

Yet it is Lyuka's image, as it appears in Pavel's reminiscences, that helps Laurence to realize that such perfection is possible "with everything together -- love, success and fame." And with this revelation, life becomes easier for her. For both Laurence and Pavel, the image of Lyuka is a consolation. Laurence feels that something heavy has fallen off, shifted within her, and that deep inside where it used to be dark and stuffy, there is now breeze and sunshine. Consolation: Lyuka had searched for it many times in her life. But she herself had never succeeded in being a consolation to others; not even to her mother, who had sent her to an aunt after her sister Vera's death.

She remembers that time as "dark, bitter grief..." when she "felt like a fox running through an empty field, where a wolf might stand behind each bush and a hunter -- behind each tree."

Marriage brought her protection and consolation, evoking feelings of gratitude and tenderness toward her husband, a broad-shouldered man with kind, strong hands.

Much later, abandoned by Rivoir, she looks for and often finds consolation where she least expects it: here with the actress Arlette in Venice, there with Guéraint; and even with a chance acquaintance, a Soviet tourist to whom she confides her sufferings at Rivoir's undeserved cruelty ("I don't want a child from you... even if it is mine.")

When, still later, she telegraphs Pavel, to "come immediately", she is moved by a craving for consolation in her unbearable loneliness. She is sure Pavel would understand and forgive everything.

Loneliness. This word is repeated in this novel almost as often as "happiness" and "love." Even while driving in a car with Rivoir, "...a lonely tree... disappearing from sight, sinks into memory, as the pain of loneliness."

The fear of loneliness torments her even at the height of her passion and happiness, as she lies in bed at the sight of sleeping Thiery. "...From the icy ceiling, deep melancholy looks into her shattered, defenseless heart... She can hear her own breathing, her loneliness."

Later, abandoned, she struggles with the decision to trace her husband and appeal to him. Her feelings in turmoil, she keeps repeating to herself: "...not to be alone, only not to be alone. To leave the solitary confinement of my room, my consciousness, my grief. To find friendship, compassion, a warm, outstretched hand..."

In order to better understand the heroine's turbulent state of mind, one must know something about the events that preceded Lyuka's tragic end.

The novel begins with the unexpected promise of fame, with all its temptations. Waiting for her second meeting with Rivoir, she already feels "her old childhood desires," awakened after a long-lasting nightmare, joyfully swarming in her heart, in her mind, in her whole body. "And she suddenly realizes that this new, gay, impatient expectation is not only thirst for life - she is falling in love with Thiery Rivoir. Now nothing can darken this new, no, *first* happiness in her life..."

And the expectation "is so eager, acute, prickly like an owl, like a porcupine. She constantly keeps stumbling over it, it stings and causes blood to run..."

Until this point we have seen the early Lyuka. Running into the house with the signed contract, she excitedly spreads the money into a fan shape on the table and hugs her husband. "What a life we're going to lead, Pavlik... get dressed quickly, quickly, there are so many things we can buy now for me and for you..."

The description of their shopping is a new poem about things that always had had a naughty, expensive air and seemed to say: "Move on, don't stop, you can't afford us anyway." Now the same things have become as "accessible as the women of Montmartre."

Lyuka is a poet. She expresses feelings and thoughts with poetic images, transforming the most prosaic things and events into poems and songs.

While sitting under a hair dryer, its noise makes her imagine she is in an airplane. "She flies above the Earth, above her destiny... there is her former life, so much blue colour... skies, lakes, mountains. This is peace... she used to call it boredom. The days were tall, blue... Very spacious. And everything breathed, sang in life's warm fascination. Now her days heavily tower over each other, lying in heaps, flattened, crushed like carriages after a railway collision... now her days are overcrowded with anxiety, work in the studio, and the joy of being in love."

And still, this is happiness, even though clouded by the necessity of hiding the true source of it from Pavel her husband, and inventing excuses for coming home late at night.

One day she returns incredibly happy. "I want you to be my wife." It was not Thiery's plea, but his order, his decision. And yet she keeps delightedly repeating this sentence in various keys to herself. She could even sing it triumphantly, were it not for Pavel. How could she tell him?

"She feels weak, mean, and cowardly in her happiness. Yet it is still not the stage of happiness," that is "cruel, insane, militant, when only the "I" is important, when one is totally indifferent to others. This is still compassion, kindness, generosity -- "Let everybody be as happy as I am."

She tries to make Pavel happy by promising him a trip to the Riviera after the film is completed, yet cannot help feeling deeply guilty, looking at him peacefully and trustingly asleep next to her.

The last days before she leaves him for Rivoir, she is so affectionate and attentive to him, that he, looking radiantly happy, says: "it is like Christmas. When I feel very happy, it always seems to me that at any moment they will light up the tree..."

No, Lyuka is not heartless. She succeeds in spending the whole day and evening with Pavel, and he enjoys every moment of their time together, not knowing that it is the last carefree day he will ever spend with her.

As for Lyuka, she now lives through a time, when "the world around her... again has become the background for her happiness. She would pick up objects as if caressing them, would smile at people as if wishing them good luck." Now Thiery wouldn't part with her even for an hour. He wants to have a son with her, and she, who had always feared motherhood "more than typhus, more than poverty, more than fire," agrees. For him, she would gladly suffer the "pain and disfigurement of childbirth."

But the evening of her greatest bliss turns out to be the beginning of many days of fear of losing her happiness, of pitiful attempts to hold on to it and, finally, of the realization of hopeless loneliness.

Suicide or accident? Neither the reader nor the novel's characters can answer this question with certainty, since the author gives sufficient hints that could support either. Here we see Lyuka with Thiery on the top of a mountain: " 'I am very happy at this moment', she said. Then, with a sigh: 'What if I slipped and tumbled down?' But this was only a thought, vaguely suggested by a seagull's zigzagging flight."

Then we meet her on a train, returning from Venice after the final breakup with Thiery. She is heading for the dining car. "The wind, space, rattling of the wheels and speed... What if I gave in and slid down on the roadbed, under the wheels?"

But later, when she receives Pavel's telegraphed answer, "Arriving tomorrow", she is excited by the hope for a new life; after all, she is only twenty-one, and it is not too late. "She no longer wants fame... she dreams of a house, a son... her Pavlik is kind and life will be good again." If only the twelve hours until he arrives could fly by quickly! And she heads for Versailles after a dinner (with wine) to shorten the waiting.

In the automobile she feels slightly dizzy: "A bright moonshine... that makes her eyes blink... To live! To be alive as long as possible... She cannot turn her eyes away from the moon."

This whole page is flooded with so much pure poetry that it is almost impossible to choose a quotation. "She sees her life like a tree, shedding leaves -- years, three, five, eight. She thinks of the many things ahead of her -- grief, joy, excitement... The road is white, framed with big, blossoming apple trees... it ascends straight into the sky... So this is what Venice looks like. In the clouds, under a black bridge, sails a blue Venetian moon. And still lower... somewhere far away in Lyuka's nursery, between rows of toy trees... she sees a toy automobile rolling along. Then, it makes a turn, collides with a tree, and stops... Like a bird from a cage, a blonde-haired doll flies out of the car window and hits the trunk of a tree..."

We see that Lyuka's thoughts and feelings during the last hours of her life are as full of contradictions as her whole nature is and as Odoevtseva's poetry is ("I'm so sad, I'm so merry...") Thoughts about her unborn son, her ex-husband Pavel, a house, and a new life are forced out by the vision of a bridge in Venice, on which she and Thiery are embracing: "Never to separate. To be with you, Thiery, forever."

* * *

One Year In A Life*
("God Zhizni")

When I met with Odoevtseva in Paris in 1980-81, I asked her about *One Year in a Life*. Yes, yes, Odoevtseva said enthusiastically, she knew how the novel was to end; she would set about finishing it now. But after twenty five years, the details of the plot and character were hazy in her memory. Could I read it aloud to her, since her eyesight was no longer clear? So I read the novel aloud to her twice, as she strove to feel once again the poetic style of the work.

Several years later, now back in Leningrad, she was still promising to complete the novel, but she never did.

Like Odoevtseva's earlier novels, *One Year in a Life* deals primarily with romantic teenagers or young women whose daydreams lead them into a collision with real life. The male characters only form the background for plot development and the resolution of conflict; they are mere sources of the female joy and suffering that Odoevtseva explores.

This is a novel of acute conflict. The basic conflict of the eternal triangle is heightened by a rivalry between sisters, as well as a conflict between ideologies: the husband's rival is a Communist.

---

* "One year in a Life" remained unfinished. It appeared only in Periodicals: "Novy Zhurnal" and "Vezrozhdenie" in 1957.

This is the first time Odoevtseva introduces an ideological note into her novels. In the previous ones, *The Angel of Death*, *Isolde*, and *The Mirror*, the relations between the characters remained within a purely personal frame. World events, such as the Russian revolution, were glimpsed only dimly, when they affected the heroines' personal lives -- for instance, characters mentioned in passing, the execution of Lyuka's father or the killing of Lisa/Isolde's father by Soviet sailors.

Politics remain a minor theme in this book too, but they remind us of Odoevtseva's other novel, *Abandon Hope Forever*, which strikes out in a new direction.

The emotional range of the two sisters who are the protagonists of *One Year in a Life* does not extend beyond infatuation, love, and passion. These feelings, which dominate their youth and their mature years, do not often lead to happiness. Their mother was capable of abandoning her children; one of the daughters, born of passion and jealousy, is led by the same emotions to hate and slander her sister; love for a man even makes her willing to commit a crime.

Kira and Asya live in France. They suffer not only the poverty of émigré life, but the fate of orphans. They lose their father at an early age, and are then abandoned by their mother.

At sixteen, Asya falls in love with Mikhail Skaryatin ("Misha"), a summer guest in their "private boarding house". His behaviour towards her gives her every reason to believe that he reciprocates her feelings. It wounds her all the more deeply when he chooses as his wife her older sister Kira, who is skinny and has a shaven head after a bout of typhus. Asya does not share her inner life with anyone and Kira never finds out about Asya's love for Skaryatin. She interprets Asya's despair at the newlyweds' departure as mere reluctance to be left alone on the farm.

Yet grief makes Asya lose her appetite, her sleep and powers of reason: " I'll lose my mind, I'll die. No, I'll kill her. Kill her..." And she does, in fact, go so far as to put rat poison in Kira's pastry; but murder is averted when a dog eats the pastry instead.

She then makes Kira swear to take her with the couple to Paris: "...If you don't keep your promise, you'll be cursed and die in terrible torment." Later, in her letters to Kira she threatens to poison herself. Living in Paris and visiting the couple often, she so skillfully hides her love that no one notices it. But when Kira one day turns to Asya in distress, Asya suddenly becomes an unscrupulous rival. She seizes the chance to oust Kira as the wife of the man whom she, Asya, has never stopped loving.

Kira tearfully confesses to her sister that she has been seduced -- a single incident, which she sees as an accident. Expecting help and compassion, she is startled at her sister's reaction: "This was not Asya. This was a grown up, skinny, pale woman with the face of a religious fanatic, distorted with cruelty." Asya insists that Kira leave home immediately, without explanation, convincing her that her husband will never forgive her and might even kill her.

To Skaryatin, who almost loses his mind with grief, she tells a different version: Kira, she claims, has been unfaithful for almost the whole year and decided to leave with her wealthy young French lover, although Asya has begged her not to.

Asya hopes that her tale will destroy Skaryatin's love for Kira. But he reacts quite differently. Left alone during the first few days, he succumbs to grief, rage and despair; he even attempts to commit suicide. Then he begs Asya not to leave him.

Asya's wish, one would think, is fulfilled. Now it is she, not Kira, who will see him off in the morning, greet him in the evening and take care of him. So far the theme of the book has been a classic one throughout world literature and folklore: the perfidy of a woman, or a man, who tries to win the loved one by slandering the rival. But Odoevtseva develops her own variation of the theme. Gradually, Asya becomes convinced that Skaryatin still loves Kira and is waiting for her to return. Guessing his thoughts and wishing to see him, if not happy, at least less depressed, she begins talking to him in the evenings about Kira, about her habits, their childhood years together, their innocent pranks. She is glad when her stories make him smile. She begins to idealize their common past, leaving out the darker side such as their longing for their father, their mother's departure, and their dismal life on their aunt's farm.

Reminiscing about Kira, Asya involuntarily imitates her voice when quoting her words or little songs. As a reward she hears him say: "How charmingly you sing !" She reads in his eyes that he likes her imitations of Kira. But little by little she feels herself enveloped by "something disgustingly foreign, something fluffy, lacelike, something romantically flashy, melting... Kira-like." The imitation of Kira more and more often ceases to be an imitation. Asya is no longer always able to define the demarcation between Kira and herself.

Asya had always preferred simple, comfortable clothes and shoes, whereas Kira liked to wear flowing, wide dresses and elaborate hairstyle with bows. But when Skaryatin looks at Asya's flat shoes and comments that she has "feet like those of a soldier", she puts on "giddy" high heels. That day marks the beginning of an almost conscious transformation of Asya into Kira's double. Despite her disgust, she buys silk dresses with bows and belts to match the shoes. She begins to lose control over herself and is now at the beck and call of objects.

She suffers and despises herself. ("I'm a rag, and good only for making a stuffed figure of Kira.") But despite this, she takes another step in order to please Misha. Since he once said that dark hair doesn't become her, she swiftly turns into a blonde with pretty locks just like Kira. Alone, she breaks into tears, but his delight in her new look makes her forget her tears and obediently dress in Kira's suits and little hats. "After all, it wasn't that difficult to smile absentmindedly and cheerfully... to utter meaningless words... to shift grief into the future and cover it over with fragments of laughter, as light as snowflakes."

When as a child Asya had been asked "Who would you like to be?" she had always answered "Asya. Just Asya." How is it that she is now divided? No, even worse: Asya has almost disappeared. She looks, walks, dresses and laughs like Kira -- she has almost become Kira... Almost. "A flare of shame, like the flame of a match, lighted up a corner of her memory, causing a moist warm spasm in the depth of her body...''

Only once after Kira's departure does Asya become Kira completely -- though it happens in the darkness and when Misha is drunk. Yet Asya considers the incident "the one and only happy hour of her life".

Drunk and desperately longing for his wife, he comes home in the evening to see Kira -- or so it seems -- sitting on the steps of the veranda. Overjoyed, he carries her into the dark room and showers her with caresses. When he comes to himself and finds not Kira but Asya next to him on the sofa, he is at first frightened, and whispers: "Forgive me, Asya, I was drunk." Minutes later he is again lamenting his grief.

Neither he nor she ever mentions that incident. It is as if it never happened. Yet when one day she hears him pacing up and down his room "above her, almost stepping on her," she gets up and, looking in the mirror, says to herself: "This is I, Asya. But if it can't be helped, I'm ready to be Kira." And she goes upstairs into his room. This marks the beginning of a relatively happy life for the three of them, Misha, Asya and the ghost of Kira. Yet, as Asya watches jealously, the ghost takes over. Any mention of Asya disturbs the harmony and displeases Misha.

For her this deception becomes a torment. Reminiscences become confused: which are Asya's and which Kira's? She fears that she will lose her mind. When he showers her with signs of tender affection she is happy, yet still tormented, knowing that his love is meant for Kira, for whom she is just a substitute.

All this leads to the decision to tell him that she cannot go on with a double life. No longer can she steal Kira's image. She wants once more to be only Asya for him and for everybody else. She suffers, hesitates, postpones the day; but remains firm in her decision to tell him the truth. Should she not dare, she thinks, she will poison herself ("for this I'll find enough courage...")

She does not know that her "stolen" happiness and secret suffering will come to an end quite differently. An unknown woman informs them that Kira has returned to Paris. Now Asya can become the Asya of the past. But not in this house. Misha tells her to go away immediately, leaving no trace of her presence. The decision is taken not in anger -- he still doesn't know the true story of Kira's departure -- but out of love for Kira. He conveys all this to Asya with "radiant cruelty".

Odoevtseva draws Asya's portrait with rare penetration into a woman's heart and mind: the hours of her youthful infatuation; the moments of despair and readiness to commit the crime of "revenge"; and long months of tormented reflection on the need for her to transform into her rival Kira.

Asya has known only one passionate love in her life. This love is her very existence. She protects it as a secret. When she loses hope, she shares her grief with nobody and expects consolation from no one.

Who, then, is this man to whom she devotes the fire of her young heart? For whose sake does she live through tortures of disappointment, remorse, jealousy and fear?

Mikhail Skaryatin is described by Kira as having a high forehead, dark eyes, and a nice smile. He comes from Paris for a vacation on Asya's and Kira's farm in answer to an advertisement in the newspaper. Much later he reminisces that at first he almost fell in love with Asya, who met him at the station, but when he met Kira he lost his head: Is he aware of Asya's infatuation with him on the farm and later her secret love for him in Paris? He takes for granted all Asya's sacrifices after Kira's departure. It is hard to believe that Asya could hide her feelings so skillfully. He is older and more experienced. His blindness may be caused either by his lack of keen observation and ignorance of female psychology or by insensitivity and self-centredness. He is not a compassionate man.

When Kira has all her favourite books stored in the attic of their marital home in Paris ("Now we have better things to do..."), Skaryatin says: "You are heartless...that's the way you will dispose of me when you stop loving me." But as soon as there is hope of seeing Kira again, he does not hesitate to dismiss Asya, who has shared his loneliness in difficult times. The author of the novel, apparently has no great admiration for Skaryatin, judging by the devastating description of him (through Asya's eyes) when he is left by Kira: He sits down, but his knees continue to jerk... His pale face is motionless. There is something about him that is womanlike, distorted, old, something that is not typical of him. His face is covered with tears. He cries before her like a beggar woman. Finally, he asks Asya to leave; he wants to "scream, break dishes, hit his head against the wall... but alone, without a witness." He drinks. He smashes Kira's portrait, tears apart and scatters her belongings, tries to drown himself, changes his mind, still hoping for Kira's return, and then he drinks again...

It is at this point that he mistakes Asya for Kira. But after a frightened apology, he reverts to talking about himself, about his fear of loneliness, and he begs her to stay with him -- and keeps talking about not wanting to die.

He often reminisces about Kira to Asya. Here is his description of their first meeting: "I've never seen so much radiance in anybody's eyes... She was so touching... I felt like kneeling down before her and touching her hand with my lips, the way I would touch an icon... The feeling of her saintliness stayed with me for a long time, it seemed to me that I didn't deserve her..." Skaryatin believes that not even death will end the happiness of being married to Kira.

The reader might expect, as Asya does, that her tale about Kira would dispel this notion of "saintliness", along with his faith in her sincerity and love. But Kira's behaviour does not seem to matter to him. He cherishes his memories and dreams of her coming back to him. One has the impression that he is madly in love not so much with Kira as with love itself, and that parting with her is less painful than his loss of faith in the ideal of love.

When Skaryatin learns that Kira is back in Paris, he says: "I still can't really believe... but I'm so happy, so happy..."

He repeats this to Asya, forgetting all they have shared together, thinking about only one thing: Kira is back! What about the man who in one evening destroys Kira's harmonious marriage and changes her life? Here is how she describes him: "René Leroux has a hawklike profile, a small head and round attentive eyes, too light in colour, malicious..." During the first hour of their chance acquaintance she finds out that he is a French writer "already almost famous", a communist, an ardent admirer of Soviet Russia, and a hater of all who do not share this admiration -- first and foremost Russian émigrés.

Upon learning that she was born in France, but of Russian parents, he stuns her with his angry reproaches: "How could you remain here and not go back?.. For shame!.. Such a country!" Yet this does not prevent him from driving her away in his car after a visit with friends, where she became intoxicated on strong cocktails that were unfamiliar to her. When he later finds out that the conclusion of that evening has been "lost" in her memory, he pretends to believe her. But he drops his mask when he tires of her resistance to his advances. "Stop putting on airs... I've had enough of playing the noble knight... It's not the first time..."

Odoevtseva reports her character's words and actions without comment, leaving moral judgement to the reader. René Leroux, a writer who knows life and people better than Kira, surely understands that she is not an adventuress and is in his power only by force of circumstance. But he does not hesitate to take advantage of her helplessness. However, he confesses that because of her he has spent a terrible day: he complains about pangs of conscience although the very idea strikes him as ridiculous. He speaks with fury about Russian émigrés who wish to build the future as a "copy of the past"; he reminisces about his trip to Russia and about the Russian women "quite unlike her", but he reserves his harshest words for Russian émigré literature.

When Kira mentions that she is no longer interested in books, he calls this a "fear of intellectual effort... a form of narcissism and a desire to be admired." All these insults mean (as we learn from his rare explanations) that he cannot dismiss Kira from his thoughts, and he tries to meet her on the street -- all this at a time when he should be occupied with preparations for his trip to Africa with an expedition, a project he has set up with great effort. Now he fears that Kira will completely spoil the prospect of this trip.

Meanwhile, fearful of Asya's threats and of being killed by her jealous husband, Kira comes to René seeking his advice. He decides that the best solution would be for her to go with him to Africa.

Here the author leaves them for a time, and we never find out just what René and his expedition were doing in Africa. However, much later we learn that in Africa he was capable of being immeasurably more insulting, gross, and cruel towards Kira than he was in Paris. When she mentions that she is with child, he is enraged: "And what are you going to do now? What? Just answer me, what? Don't you realize that this is the end of everything ? A catastrophe. Don't you understand? A ca-ta-stro-phe!" He scoffingly describes their future in some hole of a rooming house on Montmorency with a baby screaming all night and with diapers hanging in the kitchen. "I'm finished", he rages, "because of you. You devoured me flesh and bone... I've lost my literary talent. You've killed me." Trying to wound her even more painfully, he says he has never been in love with her; that he prefers vulgar thick-lipped girls to her kind of objet d'art; he is sick and tired of her bows, curls, and perfume, her tactfulness and skill at swallowing insults, and of her helplessness--like that of a little bird of paradise, which is nevertheless able to "swallow a hippopotamus without choking on it".

Odoevtseva finds words for René that are devastating in their cynicism, cruelty and grossness. His monologue concludes: "It would be a delight for me to destroy you by strangling your delicate, perfumed neck." This violent language intensifies the contrast with a scene that follows a few hours later. Overcome by remorse, weeping "like an African torrent", René declares his love for Kira and begs for forgiveness. "I loved you at first sight, not daring even to admit it to myself. You are so unbelievably lovely, so touching... whereas I knew only dirt and baseness. I wanted to humiliate you... to prove to myself that you're no better than the rest of us. You're an angel in whose existence I've never believed. And only today..."

René the writer, who so imaginatively wounded Kira's soul, killing her motherly feelings for the baby they had conceived, now tries with the same eloquence to convince her of his love and remorse. Outwardly Kira remains calm, and in order to stop the tearful flood of speech, she says that she is not angry with him. Yet "her stone-cold heart pumps heavily: no, no, no."

The tone and language of Odoevtseva's novel appear split between the two protagonists. The most dramatic pages are those devoted to Asya: her infatuation, disappointment, her plans for revenge and thoughts of suicide, her self-inflicted humiliation and her loss of identity. Most of the book's poetic passages, on the other hand, relate to Kira, both in her happy days and in more turbulent times. Descriptions of Kira's appearance resemble the author herself, as seen by her contemporaries. Kira's early love for books also reminds us of Odoevtseva during her time with the Zhivoye Slovo society in St. Petersburg. But here the similarity ends, for Kira has no talents or special qualities beyond her angelic beauty and love of life. Kira does not feel things with the intensity of her sister. Triumphs and successes always come easily and painlessly to her. Though fate at times inflicts deep wounds on her, she does not by nature seem to be made to suffer. A resolution generally occurs without any effort on her part.

Her first grief is their mother's trip to Italy with her second husband, which Kira refers to as a "funeral", and which indeed turns out to mark their mother's permanent departure from the girls' lives. On learning about it, Kira loses her faith in God and burns her little icon. Yet, surprisingly, she survives the separation from her mother with relatively little pain.

At that time she is deeply involved in an imaginary affair, for she has fallen hopelessly in love with a certain Fred Stone, whose photograph she saw in a foreign-language newspaper. "He had such an unusual face with eyes that made her heart jump into her throat, almost choking her..." This romance, which includes an imaginary engagement and marriage in London, ends in "widowhood" when she finally finds out that her Fred was sentenced to be hanged for killing his mother for her life insurance. Reading about it, she heard the noise of her broken lamp, like a hoarse scream, above her... but the lamp just went out and Kira couldn't even die in flames. New books and countless similar "affairs" with their heroes help her overcome the grief of her loss. But the vision of Fred's face lives for a long time in her imagination... "affectionate and loving...with a loop around his neck."

Kira's unexpected marriage to Mikhail Skaryatin, without any effort to win his heart and without enduring any love pangs, made it easier for her to forget that she was the "widow of a hanged murderer". But above all it gave her a chance to leave behind their dreary provincial town and move to Paris.

Kira soon settles into a delightful new, carefree life with an adoring husband. She stops reading books, and sees life's adversities and conflicts reflected only in the movies, which do not really move her or make her think. And then an ill-starred incident casts her in the role of an unfaithful wife. This occurence simply takes place, with none of the emotional turmoil that usually precedes an affair. True, she spends a few days in confusion, trying to remember where and how she spent five hours after the cocktail party at the house of an extravagant American lady whose portrait Asya was to complete. Odoevtseva poetically describes Kira's thoughts and feelings: "Her whole life lies like a pile of rubbish and wood chips, like a train after a collision...

She lies at night, perturbed and apprehensive... Suddenly the scream of a famished cat... neurotic, plaintive... breaks the silence... And she herself, Kira, turns out to be that skinny, mangy cat, cautiously flattening herself against the chimney, senselessly and hopelessly mewing away on the moonlit roof, searching for the lost hours, arching her spine, clambering, slipping on her scraggy unsteady legs, calling for help in a tragic voice, begging, complaining, reproaching fate... until, weakened by screams and worry, she at last grows numb and falls asleep.''

Kira tries to think of a way to explain events to her husband, to prove that she has done nothing wrong, but she sees that by doing so she would only complicate the situation. Having found no solution, she runs away without explanation.

Where could she go? Could she avert poverty by somehow earning a living? But how? She has learned no trade. All talk about the ennobling nature of work is just hollow words to her: she prefers a life of leisure and merrymaking. Ironically, she was recently reflecting on this. But now, fearing for her life, she flees to the man who has destroyed her carefree existence.

The reader cannot help wondering at how easily René calms her down. Yes, he tells her, jealous bourgeois husbands in fact do often kill their wives. Escape is her best choice. Having a passport she has nothing to worry about.

We see her already calmly looking at the bookshelves in René's room, curious about the view from his window -- ''she suddenly forgets what has happened and why she is here.'' But she is relieved by the fact that there is no need to think or struggle. A solution is found: she will go to Africa with René. Eight months and thirty pages later, when we meet her again, however, we do not find Kira changed or enriched by life in a new country at the side of a writer. Does she try to be part of his life and activity? Does she seek to learn about Africa? No, she spends her time there waiting for René to come home. That means continued idling, especially boring and cheerless because of his indifference and frequent rudeness.

Yet their drama comes to a head: she is expecting a child, and she waits for René with mixed feelings of fear and hope. His reaction exceeds her worst fears. Although his wrath and accusations later turn into tearful remorse, declaration of passionate love, and promises of happiness, Kira decides to run away again to an unknown future.

Now she is driven not by fear, but by hatred for René who has killed all her other feelings. "I must force myself to forget all that is connected with René. Forever. Completely... Simply by saying 'I hate you' I begin feeling strong, firm, almost calm..." Thus Kira manages to get passage on a ship back to France and returns to Paris.

Once again Kira is spared a long, hard struggle. Fate once more grants her protection and help, this time in the person of a wealthy religious patroness. On the voyage she shows compassion for Kira, assuaging her fears. We then see her in Paris, living in Versailles, taking piano lessons. Geraldine gradually reveals to her the blessing of another kind of love, selfless and pure, born of a desire to help others, a love that brings happiness through forgiveness and mercy. It is at this point that the novel breaks off uncompleted. The reader guesses that another Kira is being born, that Kira is entering a world where there is no room for René, or Misha, or Asya. We do not know her feelings for her unborn child. But the author has prepared a painless solution: her husband's eagerness to see her suggests that he will forgive and forget. Thus, Kira will again be surrounded by love and care. However, it is risky to predict the ending of Odoevtseva's novel. Her characters are complex and full of contradictory traits. In development of the plot, as in her style and language, she creates her own laws.

The plot as planned by the author was to take still more twists. Odoevtseva outlined to me in Paris the story line she had constructed before even beginning writing:

René returns to Paris, madly in love with Kira. She still loves him, and they are reconciled. But the young woman who seems to find her way out of every problem eventually meets with a tragic end, dying in childbirth. René returns to Africa.

Mikhail wants the child named after his beloved Kira, and he and Asya take the child to raise. They then settle once again into a threesome. But instead of Misha, Asya, and the ghost of Kira, it now consists of Misha, Asya, and the child, named Kira.

*　　*　　*

Abandon Hope Forever
("Ostav' Nadezhdu Navasegda")

This novel is dated "September 1945 - November 1946." It was thus written in the first year after the end of the Second World War. The title refers to the state of mind of the Russian people, who had hoped the victory over Hitler would bring real change to their country.

The novel was published in French in Paris, by SELF Publishers in the year 1948. It appeared in English in New York in 1949, and the same year in Spanish (Barcelona: Luis de Caralt Coleccion 'Gigante'). Only in 1954 was it made available to Russian readers in the West in an edition by the Chekhov Publishing House of New York.

The novel is a major departure for Odoevtseva. For the first time she extends her scope beyond the psyches of teenagers (*The Angel of Death, Isolde*), their striving after fame and elusive glow of happiness. Many readers, including the author's husband, Georgi Ivanov, were surprised that the principal characters were no longer women, nor teenage girls with their insatiable craving for love. The central characters this time were men, whose destinies were forged in Russia between the beginning of the century and the 1930s and 1940s. Through the prism of their emotional experience, thought and action, readers see and share the fate of the country and of its people.

Odoevtseva treats this theme from her own perspective. None of the principal characters are peasants or workers, but we do see an estate set on fire by revolutionary villagers, and we learn of the death of the protagonists' mother in the fire. When asked about all this later, the peasants gloomily turn away and assert that they did not do it, although they did nothing to prevent it.

We hear, too, the voices of city people in a communal kitchen under the Soviets: "Just look at her audacity! Such cheek! She took up the whole table and I have to stand there and wait!" We also shudder at the backstage intrigues of the ballet theatre in which yesterday's star finds herself on the street after her husband's arrest. It is a world of envy, fear and fawning, utterly unlike the noble world portrayed on stage.

In this novel, the masses play only a secondary role in the tragedy of the intellectuals. Yet this is a book about Russia in terrible times, written during years when the world had heard much about the inferno of the revolution but still did not know the whole truth about events in Russia between the two world wars.

What is unusual in this novel by a Soviet émigré is that the system is denounced not by a victim but by a representative of the government, an enlightened revolutionary who in his actions remains a devoted follower of the Party. The bitter thoughts expressed by Volkov to his condemned brother speak more strongly than a whole volume of denunciations by a convinced anti-Communist.

In her renowned ability to penetrate the human soul, the author possesses a sharp mind and has a good understanding of her country's history both ancient and modern and of the causes of Russia's tragedy.

Like other Odoevtseva novels, this one also has two protagonists who represent different types or points of view. Andrei Luganov and Mikhail Volkov are adoptive brothers. Mikhail Volkov is in some ways an anti-hero, representing views repulsive to many Russian readers. Yet through him Odoevtseva expresses her own thoughts about life, love and friendship, loyalty, war and patriotism, liberty, the Russian Revolution and the idea of world revolution.

The last time the brothers see each other is on the eve of the Second World War. Their moods reflect two principal currents of thought in those memorable days -- apprehension mixed with a secret hope for significant change, and a burst of patriotism and awareness of the duty to defend one's country despite the sufferings of the twenty years that have elapsed since the Revolution.

It is the writer Luganov who turns out to be the ardent, sincere patriot despite having suffered during Soviet times. He rejects indignantly his brother's offer to help him leave for the West during the imminent war. Volkov's prediction that the Red Army would be unable to hold back the German hordes may remind those who during the war, on impulse and suppressing doubt, left for the West. Luganov, however, had time to agonize over the situation during his sleepless nights. At the time of the German retreat, many Russians had to decide on the spot whether to stay or leave. People who had already suffered much, chose the unknown, and fled to escape further suffering.

"Betrayal of Russia? Nonsense!" argued Volkov. "You are not betraying Russia but only Soviet rule. Even if you had sworn allegiance... no oath would equal what Soviet rule has done to you and what it will still do... You will remain loyal to your fatherland... You must save your talent for Russia. It is your duty..."

To Luganov it seems like a bad dream that his brother should try to persuade him to leave for England or France when the opportunity arises. He is no less terrified to hear what to expect in Siberian exile: "You, Luganov, the best writer in Russia, will rot away slowly, miserably and shamefully..."

Having turned to God in jail, he prays that God will send him a quiet, easy death... Then, again, he hears Mikhail's voice: "Oh, how much you can still do for the glory of Russia, for her real glory..."

What hurts Luganov most is the revelation that some of his closest friends have betrayed him. After a night full of nightmares, doubts, vacillation and prayer, Luganov decides: "No, even if God does not grant me death now, I will endure everything... forced labour... scurvy... One can defend Russia even with one hand... Is this not the way to fight for these stars, for a Pushkin poem, for the whole past and future of Russia?"

But he never has a chance to defend Russia. While wrestling with doubts and conquering his fear of slow and agonizing death, his fate has already been sealed. His prayer for an easy death has been heard by God. But he is granted the illusion of great happiness: He is forgiven. He will go to Moscow where Vera is waiting for him. His books will be published again. He accepts Mikhail's merciful lies as a miracle: "Job received back his riches... but I was given more than that. Much more: I regained my childhood heart and my youth..."

Involuntarily one finds oneself following the author's manner of starting at the end and then returning the reader to the beginning of the events.

In hardly any of Odoevtseva's novels does the action occur chronologically. There are five parts to this novel. The author uses flashback technique four times, elaborating, explaining and adding to the present with a review of past events. But she does this with such mastery that readers easily follow the development of the plot, and are never confused by the time switches from the forties to the beginning of the century and back to the postwar Stalin era.

We meet the writer Luganov in exile on the eve of the Second World War. His brother Mikhail Volkov, who has managed to get Luganov's sentence reduced, arrives unexpectedly to have a serious talk with him.

Then Odoevtseva leaves the brothers with just one sentence "Their friendship began the 16th of August, 1905, on their first day in high school." Now she transports us to St. Petersburg, to the family of Professor Luganov's widow, who later becomes "Mama Katya" to the brothers. We see their high school life, their summer vacations on a country estate, their rowdy life as university students, their parties, political meetings, concerts, and reading of forbidden revolutionary writings.

We are touched by the arrest of Mikhail, a student of jurisprudence, and by his exile to Siberia. We witness Andrei's rise to literary fame, his enlistment as a volunteer in 1914 and his return to the country estate, where his mother has been burned alive by the peasant mob. Unlike Turgenev's mother who was a harsh mistress, the boys' mother was a generous woman who had always shared her sons' idealism. Her kind and noble nature is reflected in every line of her letter to Andrei at the front: "If anything should happen to me, Andrei, don't be angry at the peasants. Forgive them. Their brains are now twisted by liberty. They are intoxicated by it, and inebriated people always turn into wild animals. You have to understand them... The Bolsheviks came from the city and brainwashed them. For the sake of my memory, always love each other... as I love you both."

But Andrei, who can defend neither his mother nor Russia, and Mikhail, who is now a prominent member of the Bolshevik Party, find themselves on different tracks. Both feel the grief of their loss deeply, each in his own way.

"No, I am not with you..." Andrei once said to Mikhail. "Like Kipling's cat, I walk by myself, all alone." On another occasion he criticized the Party to his brother: "In the name of your love for a set of strangers, you even kill your own near and dear ones." Such statements were still possible in the first years after the Revolution. Later on, no one would dare say such a thing to a Party member.

Yet it is through Mikhail's efforts that the silenced writer Andrei is allowed to return to literature. Though not rejecting "official orders", he avoids politics as much as possible. His success with readers and critics and his happy marriage to the ballerina Vera Nazimova -- all this makes him forget his doubts. He does not notice what is happening around him, or perhaps he prefers not to notice. His happiness is so great that only the fear of losing it sometimes darkens his mind.

How, then, does he endure the loss of this wellbeing, when for a trifling offence he is thrown into a solitary cell? The author describes no details of the interrogations but tries to penetrate Andrei's state of mind. Not knowing the jail's Morse Code system, Andrei is totally cut off from the world. His hopes of freedom (surely Vera and his friends are trying to intercede for him...) give way to resignation, despair and, finally, a total indifference to himself and his fate.

The author devotes several pages to Luganov's reflections, conversations with himself, and dreams. Vague thoughts about God appear but are overwhelmed by reflections on death and insanity, which gradually dim his tormented mind.

Only while convalescing in the prison hospital after his suicide attempt, does Luganov realize that faith in God is a blessing, and that God's demanding love has always been with him in every work he has written. Now, if asked whether he believes in God, he would answer without a moment's hesitation: "Yes! With all my heart! As in my childhood... when God meant only kindness, only love."

Some time ago he has read through Vera's copy of the Bible and even memorized much of it, fascinated by the poetry and mastery of the English translation. Now he asks Volkov to bring him this Bible.

Andrei now thinks less frequently about Vera. Mikhail has concealed from him everything that has happened to her after his arrest. Instead, he tells Luganov that she is touring the provinces with a dance company, that she is constantly surrounded by friends, and that she is anxiously awaiting his release from jail.

In appearance, Vera resembles the characters of Odoevtseva's other novels as well as the author herself, as described by her contemporaries. She is slim and looks so fragile that a breeze could break her. Her capacity for exaltation also resembles that of Irina Odoevtseva. Surrounded by love and attention, Vera experiences success in the ballet at an early age. She meets the famous writer Luganov unexpectedly and falls in love with him. Ten years of unclouded marital happiness, together with fame as a prima ballerina, turn her into a fragile soul, totally unprepared for the harsh destiny faced by so many Soviet women of that time.

Nevertheless, when she learns of the possible arrest of her husband, Vera hides her fears, encourages him, and tries to avert danger by helping him to burn the letters of friends who have fallen out of grace with the authorities. "How brave she is!" Andrei later reflects in prison. "The wives of the Decembrists[1] must have been like her!"

Yet Vera has never had to deal with the secret police. How could she see through their tricks of interrogation ("Your husband has confessed everything")? How could she withstand the treachery and refined cruelty of interrogators who extracted "confessions" from much more sophisticated people? It is hardly surprising that Inspector Strom manages to force her to sign *his* version of the burning of the letters and extracts from her a promise not to intercede on behalf of her husband ("You cannot save him, anyway") and even to divorce him.

Volkov is not justified when he accuses Vera of betrayal ("Slut! Scum! I'd like to beat you up! I'd like to maim you") -- especially since he is familiar with the system of interrogation. But maddened by her failure to let him know about the arrest of her husband, he is incapable of reasoning logically. He keeps yelling at her:"There are no tortures! That's all fairy tales. And even if there were... you'd only spend some time in jail... Do you realize who you are and who he is?"

The cruelty of the accuser and the total defencelessness of the victim recall a scene in Odoevtseva's *One Year in a Life*, between the communist writer René and Kira in Africa. Both heroines, after enduring the humiliation of undeserved insults and accusations, not only remain unbroken but actually gain strength. But while Kira resolves to act immediately, Vera makes an unsuccessful suicide attempt before choosing to live -- albeit a life far removed from her ideals -- in the subconscious hope of taking revenge for her suffering.

---

[*] Decembrists: members of a conspiracy among Russian army officers to introduce constitution reforms. Their coup of December 1825 against Nicolas I failed.

Like all Odoevtseva's female characters, Vera Nazimova is first and foremost a woman. Transformed from an impoverished, unattractive, outwardly brutalized "former wife of a people's enemy" into a graceful, elegantly dressed and attractive young "interpreter", capable of charming any foreigner, it is understandable that she cannot remain indifferent to the privileges of her new position. For two years she has been isolated, living with callous neighbours in a communal apartment, and has parted from the theatre and her friends. That lack of human warmth left its mark on her. Now, however, people hasten to open doors for her. She reads envy in the eyes of former friends, the ballerinas in the theatre, where she is suddenly a welcome visitor. All this helps her become resigned to her position as a "guide".

But this job also holds a hidden danger. She sees admiration in the eyes of an American doctor called Ronald. His ability to intuit and fulfil all her wishes, and his gentleness, later turn into open admiration and gradually carry her away. She becomes infatuated. Moreover, she now sees a chance to escape from the system that destroyed her happy marriage, her career and her human dignity.

There is a struggle in her mind and heart between the fear of losing this hope, this love, and her innate honesty. She cannot betray the trust of the man who has fallen in love with her. The author very poetically relates this inner drama with a description of the decisive evening in a restaurant on Tverskaya Street where they are entertained by Gypsies. Their songs resound in Vera's mind, now raising hope, now admonishing silence or flinging her into an abyss of despair: "What a pity that we met so late in life".

Finally, the silence is broken. Her hope of leaving for America "on a white yacht" is crushed. The gap between Ronald's world and the one he has seen here is too great. The sudden departure of the clever American is greeted jubilantly by Inspector Strom. But for Vera, this is the first step down a road "that leads away from virtue". She has suffered punishment, despair, and attempted suicide. Now she feels she has the right to commit a crime.

We meet her again only at the end of the book, in postwar Berlin, at a diplomatic reception. She is playing the role of a banker's wife, but is a secret agent who manages to bring before a firing squad even her former interrogator Strom. Now it is her turn to instil fear in the hearts of those guilty of destroying others people's lives. Here she finds a chance to remind Volkov of his cruel treatment of her in the past.

However, the author does not portray her as a malevolent person drunk with power. Though she "lives well and very merrily", she has forgotten nothing. When speaking about Andrei, she wipes the affable smile from her face, and her genuine suffering shows through.

Though Andrei and Vera are both important in the story and each embodies some traits of the author, it is Mikhail Volkov who in my opinion is the main character in this novel. He is the most complex personality, full of contradictions. Though in the conflict between good and evil, he is, by virtue of his position, on the side of evil, it is nevertheless difficult to think of him as an anti-hero.

In his youth he was a fiery and fearless revolutionary. After 1917 he was close to the Soviet Olympus, a high executive in the secret police, later high-ranking officer in the Second World War. He would seem to have every reason to be content with his destiny. We learn from his own description about the brutal repression of well-to-do peasants. As a member of the Bolshevik Party, he obeys orders, often trampling on human lives.

And yet the author depicts Volkov as also capable of noble sentiments and actions. He remembers and reveres his adopted mother throughout his life. Even after her death his love for her is so deep that there is no room in his heart for any other woman. He also remains faithful "unto death" in his friendship with his adopted brother Andrei, although the latter turns his back on the Revolution. He saves Andrei's life repeatedly, even risking his own position in the process.

In energy, erudition, intelligence and perspicacity, Volkov is superior to the writer Luganov, the idealist who proves incapable of either attacking others or defending himself. Volkov, however, can critically analyze not only his own actions and mistakes, but also the failings of the whole system, which elevated him to the very top and is also ready to destroy him for his cleverness, success, and popularity among the soldiers.

Volkov is a deeply unhappy person. He has lost faith in serving his people but continues to follow the party line and obeys the leader according to the principle of "I cannot act otherwise". Even when he is commanded to do the unthinkable -- to kill his beloved brother and friend -- he replies with the customary "It will be done". The reader, however, cannot but feel his torment: "Oh, if only one could forget!" he cries out when Vera asks him several year later whether he remembers Andrei.

But there is a hidden risk in sympathizing with Volkov, especially for Western readers. His theory about the history and nature of the Russian people could hardly meet with the approval of either Russian readers or their present government. On the other hand Volkov's thoughts about Gorky, Esenin, Maiakovsky, Meyerhold, Zinaida Raikh and the "intelligentsia" in general -- thoughts that represent a revolt against Soviet rule -- do not sound at all rebellious to readers in the West or to many Russians.

This part of the novel is saturated with so many thoughts, sometimes contradictory, on so many topics that to analyze them would take a major article in itself. So I will simply present without comment some of Volkov's assertions in his confession to Andrei in the first chapter of Part Five, in order to give readers some sense of Volkov and of the intellectual territory he covers.

Volkov has devoted all of his life to the Party and the Revolution. However, now he can no longer believe the world will be saved by the Russian Revolution that "substitutes Evil for Good and destroys without creating. Evil evolves and changes its form, but never its substance. A revolution, like the culminating point of a sickness, is short-lived. But with us that culminating point has turned into a chronic illness. Like a gravely sick person, Russia continues to suffer in crisis and is unable to get well. And the Revolution that Russia will bring to the world will bring suffering, only suffering... The Russian people are the cannon fodder... they'll be pushed ahead over the still smoldering ruins, over the still open graves..."

He remembers how even true Party members were horrified by the ferocity of the experiment in collectivizing the peasants. But when they protest, "You cannot do it this way", the "wise" leader calmly answers: "You cowards! You're afraid to kill a few cockroaches!"

Volkov also predicts that the government will change its attitude towards the Jewish question, even to the Protocols of Zion. He forsees a struggle with "Jewish Fascism".

He also speaks of faith, disappointment, war and patriotism. When Andrei expresses his wish to defend his country, he says: "Do you really know what your country wants?.. Isn't it possible that a father will whisper to his son as he goes to the front: 'Surrender to the Germans. They will liberate us from the collective farm'?"

When expressing his compassion for the Russian people ("there is no people on earth more unfortunate"), Volkov summarizes Russian history. "Come and rule over us." The Russian people have voluntarily given up their liberty, says Volkov. But he does not expect changes to come from the Germans; he is convinced that Russia will win the war. But then "we will appeal to the whole world: Help us!"

In this conversation, which becomes almost a monologue, Volkov finds passionate words that are full of painful doubts. Quoting Pushkin's "We are lazy and incurious", he adds: "indifferent and forgetful... The only people that doesn't love or remember its own past... a people that lamented and wept only about the Tsars Ivan the Terrible and Peter the Great..." Volkov goes on to predict that the people will also remember the "Tsar" who is causing their present suffering.

He speaks bitterly of Russians adopting everything from abroad, "from their court ceremonials to their revolutionary ideas." Always fifty years behind, we Russians "distort what we have adopted beyond recognition and then pretend that the distortions are our distinctive traits... And still -- we are a deeply original people... strangers on this planet...We are at the same time with God and the Devil... Evil is sweeter... but God also possesses an irresistible magnetic force for the heart of a Russian. Our Holy Russia had so many martyrs and hermits. But most commonly Good and Evil hold equal sway in the Russian soul..."

Volkov remembers how he adored the Russian people in his youth. "No world literature is permeated with such idealization of the people as ours... The Revolution dethroned the mouzhik, destroying the legend of his saintliness and wisdom." He describes the Soviet government's cruel experiments on the people: "They would cut the living flesh, break bones, and put them together again. They were observing 'whether a leg could grow on the chin'."

In Volkov's thoughts about the Russian people there is a mixture of love, admiration, compassion, accusation and, occasionally, of destructive criticism. On the other hand, Volkov has, if not an interlocutor, at least a listener in the person of Andrei Luganov, the writer who also thoroughly knows his own people. Does he demolish Volkov's arguments? He very rarely interrupts his brother's monologue with remarks and questions: "Does that mean that we Russians are not even human beings?" Or: "No, no, that's not right. You are way off the mark and you're talking nonsense..." Answering the accusation that Russians "love to destroy" and that they "take delight in destruction", Luganov quotes Bakunin: "The passion to destroy is a creative passion". And he adds: "It is one of the forms of inspiration, well known to creators. That is the moment when one thinks one has reached perfection and wants to dissolve in that perfection, soar up to heaven and fall in a cascade of stardust."

If Luganov's arguments seem weak, we must remember that he was listening to Volkov with only one ear: his thoughts kept reverting to his promised return to Moscow, to Vera, and to his literary fame. Andrei was hardly concerned with discussions about the history of the people and the country, although he felt ashamed at not being able to share in Mikhail's suffering and his agonized reflections.

The author apparently needs this confession to explain and excuse the change that takes place in Volkov after Luganov's death. This same Volkov, who has doubts about the Soviet power he continues to serve and about the Russian people of whom he remains a part, not only helps to defeat the enemy but becomes the idol of his soldiers ("for Victory, for our 'Volk'!")* He treats them with kindness, takes an interest in their families, and feels sorry for them "because they were dying so submissively... so simply, like birds, like trees".

This new Volkov now discovers value in things he had once ignored: great literature and music. He also discovers in himself a new ability -- to be afraid. Thus, on returning from postwar Berlin to Moscow "by recall", he asks himself: "What should I be afraid of? I am afraid of everything. I am afraid of what I have done, afraid of what they'll do to me, afraid of the past, afraid of the future... I am afraid of the absurdity to which I have devoted my life and which will soon finish with what remains of my life. I am afraid of all the sacrifice I have made..."

The author affords the reader a chance to fathom the soul of a human being who does not know how to pray in the face of death, who knows that his death will be "ignominious and painful... and that he cannot expect the miracle of resurrection".

Volkov even thinks of shortening the wait for death by putting a bullet through his own head or by jumping from the train. But he soon realizes that the habit of obeying commands from "above" does not permit him to interfere with the order of things.

* Volk (and the surname Volkov) means "wolf".

While the train is approaching the Russian border, Volkov's thoughts fly to Pechorin, the hero of Lermontov's novel, *Hero of our Time* ("Geroy nashego vremeni"), whom he has always considered the cleverest and most perspicacious person of his time. "It seemed that there, far on the Russian side of the border, winter still reigned. A heavy wintry sky hung heavily over the snow covered steppe... and in that low sky he very clearly saw the black inscription: 'ABANDON HOPE FOREVER'."

On The Banks Of The Neva
("Na Beregakh Nevy")

On arriving at the Paris suburb of Gagny in September1958, Irina Odoevtseva (now a widow) was asked by the poet and critic Yuri Terapiano: "What are you writing now?" She answered: "Nothing! I'm not writing anything and will never write again. Finished! Not another published line ever!" Fortunately, she did not keep her resolve, and did return to literature.

Although she repeatedly asserted that only Yuri Terapiano's faith in her talent, his power of persuasion and his friendly interest in her writings made her change her mind, the reader knows that sooner or later Odoevtseva was bound to resume writing. This does not mean that we should not share her gratitude to Terapiano so warmly expressed in the second volume of her memoirs. To him goes the credit for having discovered her outstanding talent as a memoirist after her very first article, with its recollections of Nikolai Otsup. Listening to her reminiscences about life in St. Petersburg in the 1920s, and noticing her phenomenal memory, Yuri Terapiano gradually kindled her desire to revive the past, along with memories of all who had formed an integral part of her youth.

Now Odoevtseva was no longer depressed by the smallness of her room in Gagny. She was carried back to her beloved St. Petersburg, to the spacious (though not always heated) halls of the Institute of *The Living Word* ("Zhivoye slovo"), to the

House of the Arts, to Gumilyov's literary studio. Once again she dreamed of becoming a poet and only a poet. She recalled the times when, though often hungry, she was always merry; when she used to carry an armful of flowers; when she met a real poet for the first time, when... This was how the memoirs *On the Banks of the Neva* were born.

Of all her prose books, this is the most poetic. The reader cannot fail to hear her voice with its capricious changes of mood from exalted to sad, from carefree and merry to melancholy and meditative.

The enchantment of Odoevtseva's memoirs, apart from their poetic language, lies also in the fact that she does not dwell on her own emotional experiences and avoids the self-admiration so typical of the memoirist. As she rightly says in her Introduction, "I write not about myself, nor for myself, but about those whom I had the good fortune to know on the banks of the Neva."

Alongside the masterful, truly Rembrandtian literary portraits of Gumilyov, Bely, Mandelstam, Sologub and other contemporaries, there are only a few lines about Odoevtseva herself dispersed throughout the book. Nevertheless, we still see her through the eyes of her contemporaries. We hear her voice and laughter not in monologue, but in the avid questions she showered on Gumilyov and later on Georgi Ivanov about the poets of that time. Indeed they often asked where her insatiable curiosity stemmed from.

Odoevtseva's innate shyness, hidden by self-control and a worldly self-assurance (especially when reading poetry), made her a silent and attentive listener -- a rare and valuable quality noted and appreciated by her contemporaries. Gumilyov once commented how hard it was to find a good listener, and added: "As for me, God has sent me your ears always ready to listen." Andrei Bely later came to the same conclusion.

Some readers may attribute Odoevtseva's reticence to her youth and lack of experience. After all, what could she contribute to the conversation of Petersburg's literary stars? But in fact her mind and talent were often undervalued even by people who knew her well, such as Gumilyov and Georgi Ivanov. Thus, Georgi Ivanov, struck by the mystic depth of her first ballad, kept repeating: "Did you write it? Really you? You yourself?... Forgive me, but looking at you, I somehow can't believe it. It is really remarkable..." His phrase "looking at you" partly explains such erroneous views of Irina Odoevtseva especially in her youth. Against the grey background of the post-revolutionary, starving city of St. Petersburg she stood out not only with her beautiful oval face and radiant grey-green eyes, but also because of her bourgeois clothes (mostly from her late mother's wardrobe), because of her youthful enthusiasm bordering on exaltation, and her ability to inspire gaiety in others. All this most likely prevented other people from seeing the true face of Irina Odoevtseva both in St. Petersburg and later in Europe. She looked so youthful that even five years after her marriage she was sometimes barred from entering a casino.

Her first lecture, at a literary evening of the "Green Lamp" held in the house of Merezhkovsky and Gippius, impressed all the members of the circle. Even Merezhkovsky found it brilliant, and confessed: "I did not expect..." Fortunately, readers who now know her works -- lyrics, novels, ballads and memoirs -- can judge her more fairly.

Odoevtseva was an innovator in the genre of memoir, both because she focused on others and because she worked freely in her own way without following established canons, creating colourful mosaics from the materials found in the magic box of her memory. She naturally preferred the sparkling precious stones, but she did not avoid the dark, gloomy ones that reflected a character's unappealing traits or tragic destiny.

Unconcerned with the judgement of future critics and literary scholars, she leads readers of every generation to the banks of the Neva and revives for them all those figures to whom she wished to "grant immortality", as she says in the foreword to her book.

Not all Odoevtseva's portraits are painted with equal inspiration, however. Her own husband, Georgi Ivanov, receives sketchy treatment in *On the Banks of the Neva,* perhaps because he formed part of her own life. Yet the very briefness of the sketch engraves his image in one's mind: the forelock of dark hair, the very white teeth, the elegant clothes and immaculate white collars, the quick wit and resourcefulness. (A more detailed portrait of him is given in her second volume, *On the Banks of the Seine.*)

The portraits of Bely, Sologub, Mandelstam, Blok -- and, of course, of her teacher Gumilyov -- remain indelibly etched in the reader's memory. In this book the voice of Odoevtseva sounds so youthful, so utterly sincere in its admiration and enthusiasm, that one forgets that the book was written many years after these meetings took place.

ALEXANDER BLOK

What, then, were Odoevtseva's impressions of the literary figures of her youth?

Take Blok. He always impressed her as a demigod. Though her shyness prevented their getting closely acquainted, she always considered even the briefest meeting with him an important event and avidly absorbed every story about him. She admitted that it was not her teacher Gumilyov but Blok who exerted the greatest influence over her. However, this reverence does not impede her recalling Gumilyov's criticisms of Blok.

Though recognizing the genius of Blok's poem *The Twelve* (Dvenadsat), Gumilyov understood those who never forgave the poet for the contents of the poem, and he even suggested that Blok should have written another, "Anti-Twelve". The poem *Retribution* ("Vozmezdie") he called a "true retribution for former success". But, while envying and (not always fairly) criticizing Blok, Gumilyov could talk about him for hours and could quote his lyrics and epic poems by heart. Unwittingly, in fact, he was conquered by the muse of the man he called a "German romantic of the first water but still a deeply Russian and even national poet".

If Odoevtseva learned from Gumilyov about Blok the poet, she learned about his matrimonial tragedy from a long "conversation" with Andrei Bely (or more accurately, a monologue by Bely) during a chance meeting in the Summer Garden. Describing Blok's kindness, nobility and fortitude in the conflict between love and friendship, Odoevtseva also shows us the character of Andrei Bely: still full of admiration for Blok, and in a fit of self-castigation, Bely apparently blamed his own treachery and betrayal for the loss of his friendship and for the poet's death. Yet neither Bely nor Gumilyov expressed so convincingly the cause of Blok's death as did Blok himself in a speech commemorating the 84th anniversary of the death of Pushkin: "Pushkin was killed not by a bullet but by the lack of air".

Applying these words to Blok's destiny, Odoevtseva quotes his own words: "Though still alive, despondent and tormented, I still can breathe, yet I can live no more."

OSIP MANDELSTAM

In portraying Osip Mandelstam, a man utterly unlike Blok both in his poetry and in his private life, Odoevtseva avails herself of all the shades of his character as a poet and as a human being: "He glanced at me with the sparkling eyes of an angel. And it suddenly seemed to me that through them, as through clear water, I could see the depth of his poetry..."

Mandelstam is often described as looking like a caricature. Odoevtseva convincingly refutes this view through her own detailed description.

Once, speaking of himself, he quoted Blok: "I carry within me, like any poet, the healing venom of contradictions."

His unusual erudition was coupled with a great modesty and a reluctance to show off his knowledge or instruct others ("Thank God, I am self-taught and proud of it"). We hear his laughter, contagious to the point of tears, about some trifle, but we also understand his outbursts of hurt when friends go overboard in their jokes. From early childhood Mandelstam had an unbounded love for the music of Tchaikovsky and would "sink into it as into the Baltic Sea". At the same time, like Ivanov and Blok, he was fascinated by the circus, and especially by French wrestling. Afraid of loneliness, he loved to walk at night on the Palace Embankment (Dvortsovaya Naberezhnaya), when "the palaces, bridges, and skies all shine and everything is white and ghostly...and you can hear the voices of the palaces... I listen and watch. Nowhere do I feel so much poetry, such wonderful, such painful melancholy loneliness".

Odoevtseva does not omit the comic aspects of Mandelstam's nature: his exaggerated fear of policemen, his helplessness in simple daily tasks ("Help! I've spilled some kerosene in the stove... I am neither a stoker nor a witch. I don't know how to handle fire..."). She remembers his overfastidious cleanliness ("the washing of hands became an obsession for him") and also his love of good food. It is easy to picture his torment in some Stalinist prison, where he perished starving slowly and painfully.

Compared to such a death, a bullet in the head would have been a less cruel fate. But Odoevtseva leaves Mandelstam in the years when he could still say: "I am so happy that I fear I'll have to pay for it." A happy marriage was his reward for his never-failing courtly respect for women.

NIKOLAI GUMILYOV

The name of Odoevtseva's teacher appears early in the book, on the third page. It is interwoven throughout the whole tapestry of Odoevtseva's memoirs, including her unexpected meeting with Akhmatova on the final pages of *On the Banks of the Neva* . But her recollection of him is neither a panegyric nor an obituary. Her descriptions are realistic, truthful, and impartial. She is not afraid to describe his faults. Precisely because of this, we see him alive; we rejoice with her in each meeting with him and we share her sorrow when she learns of his death.

Although Odoevtseva met Gumilyov practically every day from 1919 to the day of his arrest in 1921, she does not claim to know him thoroughly, so contradictory was his character. He was a traveller, soldier, hero -- but only up to a certain point. First and foremost, he was a poet. He could not be otherwise. As he said: "I was born a poet, rather than becoming one, as others do... I really was 'the child sorcerer who would stop the rain with a word'."

Gumilyov loved poetry so intensely that he wanted not only to create it himself but also to kindle its fire and help his students learn its laws so that they could begin to speak with their own hearts' language. His dictum was: "a day without a poem is a lost day".

What he especially valued in Odoevtseva was that she never tried to imitate anybody. In the studio he mercilessly ridiculed young poets of the type "like-Akhmatova," describing this as a "special kind of toadstool, such as fly agaric, that grows under the 'rosary' (a reference to one of Akhmatova's book titles, *Rosary* ("Chyotki").

Gumilyov frankly expressed his opinions about other poets to Odoevtseva. For instance, when in the fall of 1920 Mayakovsky gave a public recitation of his work in Petersburg, Gumilyov demonstratively left the hall in protest at this "collective hysteria". On his way home, however, he pensively observed: "Still, one must admit that Mayakovsky is very talented. So much the worse for poetry. What he is doing is anti-poetry. What a pity, what a pity."

Gumilyov's opinion of Mandelstam was entirely different. Once he invited some friends to his home for a first reading of Mandelstam's *Tristia* and was so entranced by Mandelstam's reading that he completely forgot to stoke the fireplace. Gumilyov asked for more and more, occasionally interspersing his congratulations with a serious analysis of how Mandelstam's poems had enriched Russian poetry.

Odoevtseva dismisses reports of mutual enmity and even hatred between Gumilyov and Blok. Despite their ideological differences, the two of them felt a mutual sympathy. For instance, Gumilyov once proudly showed her Blok's gift of a copy of his poetry collection *Night Hours* ("Nochnye chasy"), inscribed "to Nikolai Gumilyov, whose verses I read not only during the day, when I don't understand them, but also at night, when I do understand them."

Although Gumilyov was hurt at not being asked to speak at the opening of Pushkin's memorial in Petersburg in 1918, he nevertheless applauded Blok's own performance enthusiastically and called his speech "tremendous and unforgettable".

So far as the classics were concerned, Gumilyov always preferred Lermontov to Pushkin. "Pushkin's prose is the real prose of a poet, dry, exact, compact... but Lermontov's prose is just a miracle, an even greater miracle than his poetry." One of the most moving passages of *On the Banks of the Neva* describes a requiem celebration Gumilyov and Odoevtseva held on Lermontov's birthday, October 15. Later, as he took her home, Gumilyov looked at her tearful face and said: "I suddenly wish that, many years after my death, some young girl will cry for me as you are crying now... cry as for a murdered sweetheart... I wish this so very much..."

Many pages of memoirs have been written about Gumilyov by his contemporaries. But in Odoevtseva's book we hear about his life as though he were telling us about it himself. How willingly he told this attentive girl about his childhood and youth: his ambition to become a bandit chief; his morbidly selfish desire always to be first; about the first verses that "pounced" on him at age 14 in the Caucasus and possessed him forever thereafter; his high-school problems with mathematics and spelling; his surprise at managing to complete high school at all. We also learn how Gumilyov bought up and burned his own prematurely published book of poetry, *The Road of the Conquistadors* ("Put' Konkvistadorov").

From their conversation we learn also about Gumilyov's unsuccessful marriage. By the time Odoevtseva was studying with Gumilyov, he was already divorced from Anna Akhmatova and was married to Anya Engelhardt. Gradually, the drama of his two marriages unfolds before us. Odoevtseva refutes legends of Gumilyov as a sadist or cuckold, both of which versions were born of Akhmatova's verses ("My husband smote me with an ornate double whip..."; "I brought happiness to my lovers...")

Gumilyov would recall how Akhmatova used to torment him with sudden explosions even before they got married: "I'm in love with a negro from the circus... If he asked me, I'd leave everything and go with him."

Though he did not consider unfaithfulness a sin, Gumilyov never stopped loving Akhmatova. Yet her stormy jealous scenes followed by no-less-stormy reconciliations were far from his ideal of a wife as a friend and cheerful companion. According to him, Akhmatova would always find a reason to be melancholy, to complain about nightmares, to suffer from imaginary hurts, shortness of breath and insomnia, although actually she "sleeps like a log -- even cannon shots wouldn't wake her".

He considered the rumours that he was jealous of her success as a poet unjust and mean though he did admit that when he published her early poems in *Circus* during his "catastrophic" infatuation, he did not realize how talented she was. But in 1912, as he helped her put together her first collection, *Evening* ("Vecher"), he realized that she was a true poet. "And how I rejoiced in her successes! And I always wished her only the best..." As for her, right up until his death, she blamed "Kolya's tricks of revenge" for every critical review, however mild.

Gumilyov also denied the gossip that Akhmatova had been in love with Blok. According to him, they hardly knew each other. Blok used to say about her poetry: "A poet should revere God. Akhmatova reveres men."

Although he had no great liking for her second husband, Gumilyov sympathised with the man who bore the brunt of her unflattering poems: "I've turned yellow and epileptic, hardly able to shuffle my feet..."; or "A husband is for me a hangman, his house a prison..."

Odoevtseva had always revered Akhmatova. She relates these conversations with Gumilyov not to blacken Akhmatova's image or to make him look like an innocent victim, but simply to throw light on an important part of his life as a man and a poet. Without these strokes of her poetic brush, his literary portrait would be incomplete.

Gumilyov himself praised the portrait of him by the artist Shvede: "It is astonishing how truly she transmitted my face to the canvas -- even my being slightly cross-eyed. All others for some reason tried to hide this Mark of God. She, however, was able to portray me truthfully, as if turning my whole being inside out, like a glove, and show me as I really am, in outward appearance and within."

Gumilyov would no doubt have likewise admired the literary portrait of him created many years later by his former pupil. He would have been delighted that Odoevtseva remembered not only his lectures about poetry, but also his meditations on many topics, as if he had been thinking aloud, at times almost forgetting her presence.

"Only in old age or in childhood can one be totally, absolutely happy. According to Plato, love is one of three plagues sent by the gods... A poet should have either a very happy or a very unhappy childhood...but never a boring one... Death sometimes plays the important role in a poet's fame. A heroic death may put him on a pedestal. I fervently hope that God will send me a worthy and heroic death... in fifty years from now. Not before!"

In spite of his love of life, Gumilyov did not fear death. In fact, he seemed to court danger not only on the military front and in Africa, but in daily life. For instance, he liked to defy the post-revolutionary suppression of religion by ostentatiously crossing himself whenever he passed a church. Once, while reading his African poems to the sailors of the communist Baltic fleet, he intentionally stressed the lines: "I presented him with a Belgian pistol and a portrait of my sovereign".

Later on Gumilyov confessed that he was afraid. "Only an idiot cannot see danger and doesn't know fear... But one must learn to conquer fear without showing it." Still, he never imagined that death would come to him long before the elapse of fifty years. In July 1921 he organized the *House of the Poet*

("Dom Poeta") and was full of energy and artistic plans: "Lope de Vega is awakening in me... I'll write hundreds of plays." He lived according to his principle: Vivre dangereusement. "Without danger or risk", he said, "there is no life for me." Barely a month later Gumilyov was arrested. Whatever the accusation against him, we cannot imagine him repenting or holding on to life at any price. His prayer for a hero's death was heard.

Odoevtseva does not claim actual friendship with Gumilyov despite their almost daily meetings. Although he himself told her that she was "his irreplaceable and closest friend", she insists that she could not be his friend, "since friendship implies equality... I never forgot that he was my teacher, nor did he himself." In fact, Gumilyov repeated the words "Odoevtseva, my pupil" so often that once Chukovsky jokingly suggested hanging on her back a sign with the inscription "Gumilyov's pupil".

To her, however, as a "real" poet, Gumilyov was an inaccessible ideal. His merciless "tearing apart" of her draft poem at his first lecture was such a shock to her that she almost decided to stop writing poetry forever. So much greater therefore was her joy when he noticed her absence at his subsequent lectures. He apparently even approached her in the corridor of the Institute and told her: "Come next Thursday without fail."

Since he couldn't yet have known of her talent, we have to assume that he mostly remembered her looks from their first meeting. But soon her diligence in his studio must have prompted his remarks such as "You will go places... you have great abilities... you really honour me... you are the pride of my studio... I predict that you will soon become famous."

But Gumilyov was not prepared for the fame she achieved at a reception at his own home on April 30, 1920, when the poet Georgi Ivanov "discovered" her. On that occasion she recited her *Ballad of Crushed Glass* ("Ballada o tolchonom stekle"), which Gumilyov had already relegated to "the common grave of talented failures". But on hearing the exalted opinion of Georgi Ivanov and Andrei Bely, Gumilyov honestly admitted his mistake, congratulated Odoevtseva,and recited the poem by heart to Chukovsky the following day in a barber shop. The news about Odoevtseva's "Ballad" spread with the speed of lightning among poetic circles. "Now everybody and his brother will know about it," Gumilyov said.

With characteristic honesty, he also admitted his other mistake regarding the more 'serious question of her friendship with Georgi Ivanov: "I would never have thought it," he confessed, "I could have never guessed... I turned out to be a bad psychologist... I thought that you could fall in love only with Blok and that all the others were no danger to you..."

As before, he continued to speak frankly with his pupil about everything, including his own shortlived affairs. But he kept persuading her not to get married. The reader can only guess why. Odoevtseva herself explains it as his desire to keep her under his own influence. "You may fall in love as much as you wish, but don't dare marry Georgi Ivanov."

I think that among the readers of *On the Banks of the Neva* there will be quite a number of "sleuths" (to use Gumilyov's expression) who will find in and between the lines evidence that his feelings towards Odoevtseva went beyond mere infatuation. He found qualities in her that he did not find in either of his two wives or in any of the many other women with whom he had intimate contacts. To him she was a young comrade capable of sharing his sorrow and his joy, a friend in whose company he felt younger and more carefree -- one recalls their walks in the Summer Garden and his imitation of skaters; their gay, unfettered masquerade as the "English delegates" to the October festivities; their unique requiem for Lermontov, and so on. Such conjectures are supported by the sensation caused in its time by a Gumilyov's poem in which one could easily recognize his pupil: "Her bow, sitting there like a dragonfly in the golden-red tresses". But Odoevtseva always managed to avert scandal. At her request, the poem *Forest* ("Les"), originally dedicated to her, appeared in Gumilyov's *Fiery Pillar* ("Ognennyi stolp") without the dedication. She also rejected his wish to dedicate to her the poem *The Errant Streetcar* ("Zabludivshysya tramvai"), though she always regretted it, particularly because she was the first person to whom he had read this poem.

As for Odoevtseva's feelings for Gumilyov -- clearly, she was always deeply grateful to him as a poet and teacher for taking such interest in her and transmitting to her his poetic experience. She admired his energy and great capacity for work. She was always happy to meet him and was never bored in his company, no matter what they spoke about. All this encourages the surmise that had Gumilyov not been twice married and the father of two children, she herself might have become his life's companion, the one that he dreamed about.

Even years later, she could not speak of her suffering after his death: "a sacred pain. It is better to be silent about it..." But she finishes the chapter about him with some lines from her *Ballad about Gumilyov* :

The firing squad took over.
They stood him against the wall.
There's no cross where they buried the poet,

No grave-mound, nothing at all.
But his favourite seraphs came flying
To claim the poet's soul.
In heavens the stars were singing:
"Hail to you, Hero, hail!..."

ANDREI BELY

Odoevtseva devotes many pages in her book to Andrei Bely. To her he was at first a legend "a genius... resembling an angel... the hair a golden halo, the eyelashes like large fans..." Then, one day, she met him at Gumilyov's home, where she and the poets Otsup and Rozhdestvensky were to read their poetry. April 30, 1920 was a memorable day to her for other reasons. This was how she first saw Bely:
"Short, skinny. Grey hair, light as feather-down, shoulder-length.. Wrinkled pale face. And the big, light-blue, shiny eyes of a

madman... He is all motion -- the hands are extended as for flight, his sharp knees are bent, ready to go into a dance. And suddenly... he freezes in some tense, frenzied, ecstatic immobility..."

Each poem read by some poet was followed by an incoherent "verbal torrent" from Bely. Her own poem received an outburst of admiration: "Always, everywhere I was here a stranger... Instrumentation... Alliteration...That is ah-ou-yah. Aoou-ya!" And suddenly, raising his hands to the ceiling, he started singing: "AH-OU-YAH! Hallelujah! Hosanna to the Almighty! Hosanna to the Teacher!" Bely commented this way on each poet's presentation, juggling words around and never listening to anybody except himself.

How would she have remembered Andrei Bely after that evening had she never met him again? "...a true Professor Tinto from Hoffmann's fairytale, transforming himself into a big black buzzing fly..."

Then, unexpectedly, Odoevtseva happened to meet Bely in the Summer Garden. They spent a few hours together, with Bely talking all the time. And though this meeting is described to us not by a young girl with a bouquet of lilacs in her hands, but by a mature poet and master of prose, still we see the young girl beside Bely and we believe that only in the way she described could he speak of himself and his spiritual drama. The description of this meeting takes up twenty-six pages and here we see not Professor Tinto, but a man tormented by his heart's remorse: "If only one could forget. But to forget is impossible..."

Bely's monologue follows no logical or chronological sequence. His thoughts jump from the present to his childhood, then to the recent past, painfully muddled ("I would consult a dozen fortune-tellers if they would tell me my past instead of my future"). Self-justification turns into self-accusation; love and admiration turn into condemnation; enchantment and rapture into despair at the inability to understand, explain, forgive. These pages not only throw light on the mental traumas of the poet's friends, rivals and enemies, but also make up a deftly written, artistic short story on the theme of the struggle between the heart and the mind.

In these pages we see Andrei Bely whole. Here he tells us about his novel *Petersburg* : "...the best that I have ever written. It's an account of a delirium... I lived all the time in a nightmare. Horror! A phantom, a vampire formed from yellow fogs, developed by myself into a system of squares, prisms, cubes, and trapezoids... I populated my Petersburg with living corpses. I myself seemed like a living corpse..."

Then, later, after talking about Tolstoi's Yasnaya Polyana, Dr. Schneider, and the apparition of Christ which would free him of suffering ("I carry on my shoulders all the world's sufferings...I, alone!"), Bely suddenly begins talking about his childhood, about the struggle over him between his ugly father and his "beautiful mother." "Divided... I loved and hated... from childhood I have been a potential patricide." Bely's childhood also taught him to pose, to wear a mask, even when he was alone. ("I am afraid to see my own true face".)

Love, which even in his childhood was coupled with suffering, did not bring Bely happiness in later life. All the objects of his love also caused him pain: his wife Asya, Nina Petrovskaya who adored him and who shot at him and his rival Bryusov, and finally, Blok, his poems and his wife Lyubov Dmitrievna. About Blok's poems Bely said: "I rolled on the floor in ecstasy while reading them... I pictured him as being emaciated, skinny, pale... but he turned out to be offensively well, in blooming health, fantastically handsome... I fell crazily in love with him anew."

Suddenly, for Bely, Blok was no longer in the centre, nor his poems, but his "Wife, Vested as the Sun... A Beautiful Lady amid the Brotherhood of the Knights who adored her like the Virgin Mary ('Endless nights... Till dawn... Friendship Dawn... Love Dawn...')".

It would be rather risky to blame Bely for the transformation of the Beautiful Lady into a "cardboard doll" -- a doll, however, that was not bereft of temperament. ("One day she'd love me, next day she'd love Sasha. On the third day --

neither me nor him. She hated us both.'') There may be more logical explanations for the mental disturbance of Blok's wife. But the objectivity of Bely's memory is impressive: he sees how unattractive they were when they declared their love and decided to go abroad together. "And he... Such grandeur, such courage! Oh, well... I'm glad. And how splendid he looked at that moment!". We learn too that in spite of this domestic drama, Blok continued studying for his state examinations, which he passed.

It seems that in the unexpected joy of having a listener with the patience of an angel Andrei Bely opened his heart and concealed nothing. "It's so difficult to be silent. Nobody wants to hear me... A real, gifted listener is such a rarity..." He even told Odoevtseva of his attempts to commit suicide, to starve himself to death, to drown himself, and of challenging Blok to a duel. (Blok refused the challenge, saying he had no motive.)

Odoevtseva does not describe Bely's monologue in one breath. Her digressions lend reality to the whole scene, relieving the mounting tension and at the same time allowing the reader to take a rest. Bely himself in fact admitted that he could "talk people into a swoon"!

Odoevtseva's innate sense of humour helped her at the time to notice and memorize and later to reproduce the comical side of some of Bely's expressions and gestures. Fortunately, she did not share Mandelstam's tendency to giggle. She was able to restrain her laughter when in the middle of discussing his sin against Blok, Bely suddenly "meticulously examined his knee (what did he find there of interest?) 'There, it'll soon tear completely', he remarked in a businesslike way. 'There's a hole, I'll have to put on a patch.' And in the same breath he returned to his drama: 'But you cannot put a patch on the heart'..."

Here is how Bely described his decision to drown himself: "But -- fate's mockery -- there are barges, despicable, live fishponds. And everything around stinks of fish. There isn't even a place where one could drown decently." Or how his ranting caused his friend Soloviov to faint: "Bang to the ground, full length. We barely brought him back to life. He could have died."

But young Irina Odoevtseva was grateful to fate for the chance to hear details of his experiences from Bely himself. She did not laugh at him; she was touched by his accounts; she believed that he would come here every day. (In fact, as we know from other sources, Bely would often spend hours conversing with someone and then totally forget about it, later even failing to recognize his listener.)

Nevertheless, Bely's unexpected confession helped Odoevtseva create his portrait. Their meeting rewarded her and became, in a way, a second encounter with Blok; to some degree, it may also explain to readers Blok's attempts to drown his sorrow in wine.

MIKHAIL KUZMIN

With entirely different colours, but no less convincingly Odoevtseva paints her portrait of the poet Kuzmin:

Dressed in a creased and dirty tailcoat, in a peculiar, Gogol-like vest of 'little eyes and little feet'... Eyes... like two deep holes, two abysses, not like two windows widely opened into paradise... rather like two ponds abounding in frogs, newts, and snakes... the lips painted a thick, bloody red...".

One is not surprised when Odoevtseva refuses to join Gumilyov in shaking hands with him, hands that "resemble tree-roots".

When Odoevtseva hears Kuzmin reading, she realizes that he stutters ("A...a...stray dove, you flew into my heart...") but soon decides that this is the only way to read his verses. And his scrawny face, "heavily painted by age", no longer appears repulsive to her.

It was impossible to entice Kuzmin to come and hear other poets. "He shuns verses as the devil does the smell of incense. Yet he himself is such an excellent poet," Gumilyov said of him.

Kuzmin found it boring even to speak of poetry ("Poetry you have to write..."). He was much more attracted by rumours and gossip, especially of an amorous nature. We discover another of Kuzmin's strange idiosyncrasies: he was so superstitious that he would not save money, believing that to plan for disaster would bring it on.

Contrary to popular legend, Kuzmin had only twelve vests, not three hundred and sixty-five. Odoevtseva also describes another Kuzmin -- the author of poems, little ditties and *The Little House of Cardboard* ("Kartonny domik"), also a composer and performer who achieved great success in the literary salons of Petersburg, although he had no voice. "Mine is not music but *little music* (muzychka)," he once said, "but it does contain some venom."

Odoevtseva describes him at the piano: "Kuzmin lowers his head over the piano keys...ages visibly...and turns into a little old man, resembling an old woman... finically touches the keys with his desiccated little hands...He mumbles something and, rounding his mouth like a fish, swallows air ...'Your kisses are like linden honey'...He buoyantly emphasizes *kisses* . The four syllables in the Russian word for kisses (*po-tse-lu-yi*) fly from his mouth with growing explosive power and, like four gun-shots, slay the listener on the spot. Next comes the descent, sinking down to the last sobbing... half-whisper: 'Remember, there are no more violets in the summer'."

Odoevtseva also found a tactful way to describe Kuzmin's difficult adolescence, his painful struggle with his passions. According to him, he often thought of committing suicide, but continued to sin. After which he would repent and want to become a monk. He tortured his body for a whole year in a monastery. Once he prayed all night long in the church until he fainted. He was brought back to life by a kiss from an "angel", the novice Giovanni. Kuzmin left the monastery happy and convinced that the concept of sin was invented by people. From then on he never tortured himself any more. It was often said of him that he only pretended to be simple, but in reality he was very complicated.

FYODOR SOLOGUB

The complexity of poets is demonstrated by the portrait of another poet, Fyodor Sologub. Before becoming a writer, he was a teacher. His students disliked and feared him. Then he became a school inspector; from that moment on, he was feared by the teachers as well. He achieved fame and wealth not for his verses but for his prose, including *The Petty Demon* ("Melky bes") and *Death's Sting* ("Zhalo smerti"). Sologub was one of the few who could make a steady living from his literary work. His attitude to publishers was shown by his contribution to an anthology which had been planned before the revolution by Gumilyov and Gorodetsky. When he heard he would be getting only 75 kopecks per line, Sologub categorically refused to give them his better poems, and offered them lesser work instead. The gilded objects in his house dazzled the eyes. When Zinaida Gippius once exclaimed, "How resplendent, how rich!", his answer was: "I admit I like gold. I would even cover my bald head with gold but the doctor says it's unhealthy -- I would lose my talent and become envious. And I don't know of anything worse than that..."

While he was a teacher, Sologub dreamed of life in a "golden castle". Faced with a mountain of students' loathsome copybooks, he took pleasure in giving the lowest marks to "those idiots' work. Perhaps 'mommy' or 'daddy' will notice and give them a lashing."

In reply to accusations that his characters were too cruel, he confessed that he copied them from himself "...'because there are no great works without some cruelties. Without them, as without salt, a work is tasteless'." Yet the same Sologub once picked up a kitten that someone had tried to drown and tended it like a mother.

We learn from Odoevtseva about Sologub's attempt to emigrate, thwarted by the mysterious death of his wife, who adored him. She disappeared on the very day he received permission to leave the country. He stayed in the hope that she would return and even insisted that the table should be set for two people, as before. Many months later, when her body was washed ashore, his hope for her return changed to a hope that they would meet in the next world. He turned his attention to theories of the afterlife, refused to give in to despair and never again tried to leave Russia. But nobody could penetrate his inner life.

Odoevtseva dedicates quite a few pages to Sologub and the contrasts in his character and poetry. "White marbled and haughty, like a nobleman of Catherine the Great's time... he resembles a statue. A gravestone statue... A monument to himself... in undisturbed, quiet, cold, stony silence." Then, suddenly, he would begin speaking peremptorily: "A posthumous jubilee is a second burial...beneath a heavy, leaden cover. I get chills when I think of what they'll write about me... after my death. Horrible!"

But despite his firm belief in his own fame, Sologub's contemporaries did not "insult" his memory with posthumous jubilees. He died in 1927 in Tsarskoye Selo. And, to quote his own poem: "Now, there's only recollection. Then -- even a memory is no more."

But no, no! There is a remembrance and there is a memory. In *On the Banks of the Neva* Odoevtseva brings back to life many of her contemporaries, and thus we remember them forever, as she knew them.

Several dozen names appear in the book. Some she mentions only in connection with writers and poets whom she met more often. But she offers striking, unforgettable sketches of Lozinsky, Remizov, Annenkov, Otsup and others.

Thus, for instance, we see Chukovsky splitting himself in two for his inspired lectures to a small circle of listeners -- "lectures that sound like improvisations, vibrating with life, interspersed with sparks of wit and twinkling humour." Now he

imitates Mayakovsky's voice: "If you wish, I will pull from my left eye a whole blossoming grove." Then suddenly, he shrivels up, hopelessly waves his hands and says sleepily: "Pull out anything you wish. I don't care. I'm tired."
Again and again Gumilyov returns to his own past in conversations with his student. Anna Akhmatova, as part of that past invisibly is present at all his meetings with Odoevtseva. And yet Odoevtseva remembers her only meeting with Anna Akhmatova in minute detail and movingly decribes it in the first volume of her memoirs. Earlier she had seen her on the stage: "...tall, slim, even fragile, light, almost airy. And how she reads! This is not reading, it's magic..."
Unexpectedly, after her own appearance at the House of the Arts, and just before her departure from Russia, Odoevtseva found herself walking home with Anna Akhmatova and the pianist-composer Arthur Lourié, who said: " 'The night is so beautiful, it is a pity to part with it...' She took my arm in a natural, friendly way... I kept pace with her, excited and afraid to lose step... Now she spoke differently, with confidence and frankness about the feeling of safety that had never left her, not even in the darkest, most hopeless nights of the revolution... 'I knew that God was with me and nothing would happen to me...' " Having bid her farewell, Odoevtseva entered her doorway still excited at the meeting, but rushed out again, ready to run after them and to beg: " Anna Andreyevna, please, kiss me good-bye..." Suddenly she noticed that instead of two people, there were three: "to the right of Akhmatova somebody else was walking, slim and tall... casting no shadow..."
Nikolai Gumilyov, it seems, was a witness to this farewell meeting. And perhaps Akhmatova's words: " 'Still, you shouldn't leave. Kolya would not approve of it, either'..." later continued ringing in Odoevtseva's ears, even in her sleep. When she awoke, she burst into tears: "Why am I leaving? What awaits me there in foreign lands? No, I feel, I know that wherever I'm going to live, I will never be as happy as I was here on the banks of the Neva."

* * *

On The Banks Of The Seine
("Na Beregakh Seny")

The great success of Odoevtseva's book of memoirs *On the Banks of the Neva* brought her not only satisfaction but many invitations from readers in the United States and Canada. She was honoured both in émigré literary circles and in North American universities. She participated in panel discussions on literature and was interviewed for newspapers, radio and TV. Poets dedicated verses to her and students wrote dissertations about her works.

All this attention encouraged her to start work on her projected second volume of memoirs, which she called *On the Banks of the Seine*.

I remember meeting Irina Odoevtseva in Toronto and discussing the possibility of publishing this volume or part of it. She eagerly agreed to even the least feasible plan, and signed a contract with "Sovremennik [Contemporary] Publishing Inc." in Toronto. The editor, V. L. Slavin, and his collaborators were enthusiastic, and advance subscriptions were sold. But subsequently both author and editor became ill and publishing plans were dropped.

Later, when Odoevtseva moved from Gagny to Paris following her marriage, she lost the manuscript and almost gave up hope of seeing her second volume in print. I understood what that setback meant to her when I saw years later (in the summer of 1980) how much fervor and energy she invested reviving the project. By that time her eyesight was weakened by cataracts that were not yet operable, so she could not re-read the partly preserved rough notebooks. But as she listened to and commented on various chapters, she proved that despite age and illness she still possessed a phenomenal memory. She had only to hear the first lines of a chapter to recall the locale, the people discussed, the events covered, and even the newspaper in which that chapter had appeared. Odoevtseva had a gift for listening to her own work. She made critical comments and changed a word or a phrase here and there. But she also approved, without false modesty, certain apt expressions or paragraphs. We were both seized by uncontrollable laughter and reduced to tears and exhaustion when we read her pages about Teffi, and she herself exclaimed: "Bravo, Odoevtseva, she writes well!"

With his typical solicitude, her husband, Yakov Nikolaevich Gorbov, always supplied the "toilers" with tea and goodies. His ancient suitcase packed with old numbers of the newspaper *Russian Thought* ("Russkaya mysl") was a real treasure-trove. Each number containing excerpts from *On The Banks Of The Seine* was greeted by us with loud cheers. Later on the newspaper publishers also supplied us with the missing numbers. The untiring collector Dr. René Guerra helped us along with copies of the New York *New Review* ("Novyi Zhurnal") and the Toronto journal *Contemporary* ("Sovremennik"). But all these half-overgrown paths back into the past could be found only because of Odoevtseva's uncanny memory and the energy born of her newly fired hope. "Now I believe that I shall see my book published," she repeated many times.

The newly reconstructed manuscript needed editing. For example, it was necessary to remove certain redundancies that occurred because chapters had been published in various periodicals. In this the author was helped later by Professor E. N. Berg.

The sudden death of Yakov Gorbov, Odoevtseva's new illness, and a cataract operation all hampered progress on the manuscript. However, after hard work by herself and her enthusiastic friends, the book appeared in print (La Presse Libre, Paris) in 1983.

It was not the perfect edition Odoevtseva had dreamed of. She hoped someday to eliminate its flaws in a new edition. But with a new flow of energy, she now began dictating a third volume of memoirs, *On the Banks of Lethe* ("Na beregakh Lety"), which was to be marked by "total frankness about myself and others". Unfortunately, this volume was never completed.

But let us return to *On the Banks of the Seine*, a book that has been avidly read both in the West and in Russia. (Where some copies were definitely smuggled in on the first publication). Both volumes of the memoirs were republished in Moscow, by "Khudozhestvennaya Literatura" in 1988-89.

Unlike *On the Banks of the Neva*, in the second book a separate chapter is devoted to each important figure. However, these chapters are interrelated: the chapter about Balmont also reveals character traits of Adamovich; the description of the *"Green Lamp"* soirées at the Merezhkovskys in Paris contains information on Poplavsky, Teffi, and many others.

As in the first book, Odoevtseva's innate goodness and kindness do not permit her to darken the shadows on the portraits of her contemporaries; rather, she illuminates them with the rays of her love and friendship. Nevertheless, she truthfully reproduces the facts of their lives, and by reading between the lines the reader can learn what the author would rather pass over in silence or excuse. Thus, in Bunin's portrait she admits that his published memoirs pain her deeply because in them "there is neither enchantment nor pity. It sounds as though they were written with the bitter gall of old age." But immediately she tries to justify him, for "hurts, sickness, poverty and grief are poor counselors." Still, not all readers will accept the assertion that Bunin was "good, noble and generous".

Depicting her contemporaries as living beings, with their human qualities and faults, Odoevtseva invites readers to love them and thus "retain them on this earth". Will readers love them all? Or only some of them?.. Neither the author nor her critics can judge. But she helps us to understand them as human beings and in consequence brings their writings closer to us.

In the first book of her memoirs there are few references to any losses. With the exception of Blok and Gumilyov, the lives of all the others still lay ahead. Mandelstam was happily married and did not suspect the horrible fate that awaited him; Akhmatova was still in her full glory. Both those who were leaving the country and those who remained were, to a greater or lesser degree, full of hope for change.

In the second book of Odoevtseva's memoirs, however, all the heroes, excepting the author herself, have passed on into another world. Yet, though the dates of their deaths are indicated, none of the chapters resembles an obituary. While reading about Esenin, we do not think of his untimely demise, because we see him so alive at a party in the hotel. And in the case of Teffi and Aminado no death dates are recorded: we part from them as though still awaiting some new meeting.

On the other hand, to those poets who died "while still alive" Odoevtseva dedicates the most penetrating, compassionate and even remorseful words. "Dark is the lot of a Russian poet", she quotes, although these words do not apply to all of Russian poets.

MARINA TSVETAEVA

With total sincerity Odoevtseva includes herself among those to blame for the perishing of that peculiar tormented spirit, Marina Tsvetaeva.

Odoevtseva describes her first and last meeting with Marina Tsvetaeva at the home of the Ginger family. She happened to visit them with her husband, not realizing that the occasion was a farewell for Tsvetaeva. Odoevtseva's chapter about her thus adds only a few strokes to the well-known portrait of the poet, assembled from other memoirs. But the reader cannot fail to be touched by the warmth of these remarks:

Tsvetaeva's sudden merry laughter at Georgi Ivanov's jokes (which she had earlier detested); and above all, the frankness of her answer when asked on the way home whether she was glad to be returning to Russia: "Oh, no, no, not at all... But it will be better for my son there. As for myself? Émigré society has chased me away."

Odoevtseva seeks no justification for those émigrés whose hostile attitude contributed to Tsvetaeva's fatal decision to return to the Soviet Union. Her own extremely difficult family situation also needs clarification: Tsvetaeva's husband, Sergei Efron, fought against the revolution as an officer of the White Army. But later in Paris, he collaborated with the Soviet Secret Police abroad, was involved in activities against the émigrés and fled in 1937 to the USSR. (Their daughter Ariadna had returned to Moscow earlier the same year.) Tsvetaeva was left with her 12-year-old son in Paris and became completely isolated from émigré circles. In June 1939 she returned to the USSR. Two months later her husband and daughter were arrested by the Secret Police and deported. As the wife of an "enemy of the people", she was now even more isolated than in Paris.

The war, Tsvetaeva's fear of losing her son, and lack of any income forced her to join the stream of evacuees. She landed with her son in Yelabuga on the Kama at the foot of the Urals, where she hanged herself on August 31, 1941. No one knows the exact spot where she was buried.

"Dark is the lot of a Russian poet..."

Odoevtseva speaks of Tsvetaeva's poems, especially the *Story about Sonechka* which, she says, reflects Tsvetaeva herself: "young, exultant, triumphant, happy, surrounded by a triple ring of love, adoration and worship, and taking it all for granted". Odoevtseva justifies Tsvetaeva's desire for worship because she herself was capable of admiring other poets.

She quotes one of the early poems which moved her to tears:

" To all of you, strangers and friends,
(what do I care, I who knew no bounds?)
I appeal for faith,
I plead for love."

Involuntarily, one is reminded of Odoevtseva's own verses, written during her illness:

"Oh, love me, love me,
keep me on the earth.
Oh, love me, love me,
don't let me die."

This love for the earth and loathing to part from it, this thirst for the reader's love, bring together two poets whose destinies and literary creations are so different.

KONSTANTIN BALMONT

In Tsvetaeva's case the émigré community can to some extent excuse its role in her fate by pointing to the complexity of the circumstances surrounding her tragic end. But it is difficult to justify the cruelty of their contemporaries towards Balmont and Severyanin.

I believe that readers of future generations will be grateful to Odoevtseva for quoting Balmont's poems that enchanted her and her youthful contemporaries, and for describing his rise to fame and its subsequent undeserved decline.

Balmont was one of the poets who were refused a place on the ''steamship of modernity'' in a campaign launched by Mayakovsky and completed by like-minded émigrés. Balmont's ''banishment'' makes an interesting story for the contemporary reader. In 1907 he was told to leave Russia after reading his revolutionary ''Songs of an Avenger'' at several student gatherings. Claiming lack of means, Balmont refused to do so. And so, the tsarist government gave him two thousand rubles to leave, with his wife and daughter. This grant allowed him to make a round-the-world trip and to publish his ''Songs of an Avenger'' in Paris in 1912.

He was, nevertheless, allowed to return to Russia, where he delivered lectures on his new poems and his impressions of Mexico. The 1917 Revolution did not reward his enthusiasm. Suffering hunger in an apartment with "reduced living space", he took advantage of permission granted him through Lunacharsky to leave Russia "temporarily", yet he never returned.

At his funeral there were no other poets or admiring readers. His coffin floated up in the grave after a torrential rain and only with great effort could the gravediggers cover it with earth.

IGOR SEVERYANIN

Igor Severyanin also suffered from the fickleness of the public. Odoevtseva speaks of this with deep regret, although she herself did not admire all his poems and in her youth had agreed with Gumilyov and Georgi Ivanov's disapproval of his work, especially of his habit of inventing new words.

Yet, Severyanin knew real fame. Sologub, who glorified him as a great Russian poet, took him all over Russia. Everywhere Severyanin met with ebullient success and was showered with "golden rain". He later reminisced: "If I had saved the money, I would be a rich man. But I used to give it away keeping for myself only the glory. Yet even that turned out to be... devil's crocks."

He certainly did not attain the wealth of Sologub; in fact, Severyanin ended his days in Riga as a hanger-on of his Estonian father-in-law. His poetry no longer appeared in print and to get rid of him, the publisher of the Riga daily *Today* ("Segodnya") used to pay him a monthly "pension for silence".

There are Russian poets whose destiny was much more tragic. But it is difficult to find an example of a more degrading end for a poet who had known nation-wide fame.

SERGEI ESENIN

Irina Odoevtseva met Sergei Esenin only once, at Forster's, a Russian restaurant in Berlin where Russian immigrants used to meet. She and Otsup spent the rest of the evening with Esenin and his drunken "somersault companions", at Isadora Duncan's hotel, the Adlon. On the way home, Odoevtseva told Otsup: "I would have preferred not to go there... Oh, God, how sad and disgusting..." I think many readers will agree after reading her depressing description of Esenin's unceremonious brutality toward Isadora: during her poetic dancing he sat there and swore drunkenly. There is a Russian proverb: "What the sober man thinks, the drunkard reveals." Can alcohol explain away Esenin's hooliganism? Odoevtseva, as always, does not condemn but pities, though she does offer the reader her opinion to counteract the one expressed by Otsup: "It is absolutely impossible to pity him. Very few people have had such good luck as Esenin... Undeservedly... he caught his nation-wide fame by the tail like the fabulous firebird, married a world-renowned celebrity and got to travel all over Europe and the Americas..."

As though in reply to these words we hear Esenin's complaint of his sufferings. He describes himself as a naive, trusting soul, attacked in 1912 by Akhmatova, Gumilyov and "that evil wasp Gippius" -- everybody in fact, except Blok and Gorodetsky. In these few pages Odoevtseva brings Esenin back to life and invites second thoughts about the poet's tragic fate.

BORIS POPLAVSKY

Mystery surrounds the death of the young poet Boris Poplavsky, who was one of the participants in the Green Lamp ("Zelyonaya Lampa") literary soirées in Paris, at the home of Merezhkovsky. As with several other Russian writers of the past and present, there are several versions of the story: was his departure from life voluntary? Odoevtseva, who met Poplavsky frequently, argues convincingly that it was not. Like many other young talents, he was discovered by Georgi Ivanov. He conquered contemporary Paris not only with his poetry collection, *Flags* ("Flagi"), but with his brilliant oratory. He was one of the bright lights at the soirées. Odoevtseva shows him to us in action, delivering an inspiring speech on a theme that was almost unfamiliar to him.

Of his own unstable character Poplavsky used to say: "I was extremely rude to some people and cloyingly gentle with others..." He himself apparently suffered from his involvement in scandals, but his friends always found excuses for him and forgave him. Georgi Ivanov too ignored him for a whole year but eventually forgave him and even invited him to his house for a reading of Poplavsky's poems. At this reading the poet "shone, filled with joy". His recently finished novel, *Home from Heaven*, was to be read and discussed at the next reading. But this was not to be. Odoevtseva provides convincing evidence that Poplavsky's thoughts that time were far from suicide. He was, according to her, the victim of a drug addict who, in departing this life, selected Poplavsky as his "traveling companion".

NADEZHDA TEFFI

The liveliest and most humorous chapter in this book is, not surprisingly, the one about Teffi. Since she spent the war years in Biarritz, Irina Odoevtseva and Georgi Ivanov used to meet her frequently. Quite often it was in the home of a certain émigré family where everything was "tasty and plentiful" and where Teffi used to pick up words and expressions to use in her stories.

Odoevtseva remembers Teffi's ability not only to make people laugh but to enthrall them with stories. "I could be a perfect Sheherazade", she used to boast. She even claimed that she could "talk away sickness". Once she allegedly accom-

accompanied Yuri Terapiano to the dentist and distracted him while he had a molar extracted without anesthetic. Teffi could apparently dispel the most funereal mood; no wonder that she was a welcome guest in any house. She herself attributed great significance to laughter: "To make a person laugh... is just as important as giving alms to a pauper. They say that he who sleeps dines; but I say that he who laughs satisfies his hunger fully."

In pre-revolutionary Russia Teffi was already so famous that Tsar Nicholas II at first wished to include only her in the Jubilee collection to mark the 300th anniversary of the Romanov dynasty. (He was later persuaded to include others as well, with Merezhkovsky and Gippius in places of honour.) She mocked with particular malice the language and manners of the Russian émigré women who tried to make themselves look younger; but she once confessed that she was depicting herself, "something that Gogol did long ago far better than I". We recall that Sologub, too, used to depict his heroes in his own image.

According to Odoevtseva, Teffi appreciated literary success, but also liked to make other women envious of her beautiful clothes. She was very "careful" with her admirers, even with those who others felt did not deserve it. She explained this quite reasonably: "First of all, if he loves me, he is not an idiot. Secondly, I prefer a loving idiot to an over-brainy philosopher, who doesn't care for me or who is in love with another fool."

Despite the importance Teffi attached to humor, she was not entirely satisfied with her success in this field. She dreamed of writing something entirely different (we never appreciate what we possess). "Something wonderful, so as to leave a trace of myself on this earth." But readers loved Teffi's humor so much that they couldn't even imagine her being capable of writing anything serious. In her chapter about Merezhkovsky Odoevtseva describes Teffi's only lecture on an academic subject -- asceticism. It was full of Greek and Latin quotations on the myths of the hermit fathers, a subject almost totally incomprehensible to the majority of her listeners, who were accustomed to "their" Teffi. The deeper she went into the history of asceticism, the more people laughed, thinking her "erudition" was actually a brand of very fine humor. They realized they did not quite catch the joke, yet still laughed all the same "just to be sure". When she at last got through her presentation, poor Teffi sadly decided that would be her first and last public lecture.

While her little songs were greeted boisterously, both critics and readers remained indifferent to her poems. Teffi bitterly recalled Briusov's review of her book of poems called *Seven Stones*: "There really are seven stones, but they are all fakes", was his verdict.

From Odoevtseva we also learn that Teffi used to judge people by their attitude towards cats, whom she considered clever, kind, and sensitive. She wrote many verses and long poems about them. Among her heroes were cats called Romeo and Juliet, Tristan and Isolde, etc. Most likely, few people knew that Teffi suffered from neurasthenia. She would count the number of windows in a house; an odd number meant good luck. She suffered but did not like to talk about her illness. When asked, she would answer jokingly: "You see, my soul is soaked through with unshed tears... Outside of me there is laughter, 'the great dryness'... and inside there is nothing but swamp..."

GEORGI ADAMOVICH

"Of course, I'd like you to write about me, since you write so benevolently. Everyone comes off better than he actually was... You wash them clear of sins and vices... But wouldn't you like to show them as they are, in their natural ugliness?" This was Georgi Adamovich's answer to Odoevtseva's questioning after the appearance of *On the Banks of the Neva*. He even suggested that she write about everyone and everything with total frankness, but on condition that it be published twenty years after her death. Odoevtseva explained her reluctance to spice up her recollections. Readers, especially philistines, she claimed, remember bad traits more easily and willingly, and if she dwelt on these, all of her contemporaries would thus remain forever branded. But Odoevtseva does not sugarcoat Adamovich's character. One scene in a casino depicts a character hard to admire: he brutally takes away from her the money she won when playing at his request; he reveals his passion for card games despite repeated total losses; and he sighs endlessly "What anguish, what boredom!" Since her husband was a longtime friend of Adamovich, Odoevtseva knew a great deal about him. Not only did they meet frequently; at times they even shared an apartment, and of course spent hours talking "about nonsense and eternity".

We meet Adamovich as Odoevtseva first met him, at a lecture at the House of the Arts in August 1920 gracefully and elegantly dressed, outwardly resembling what Gumilyov described as a "work of art".

But she also shows him to us at home, wearing an oversized robe with his head wrapped in a lightweight blue scarf "so that the hair would stay as straight as possible". In this horrible array a passing soldier once mistook Adamovich for a woman. "Lady", he inquired, "do you need some wood chopped?" And as Odoevtseva and Ivanov exploded with laughter, the "lady" replied: "No, my husband will chop it."

What Odoevtseva adds to the information about Adamovich from other sources, helps the reader understand him. The impossibility of total frankness in their conversations she ascribes to his shyness and bashfulness, quoting Akhmatova's lines: "There is always something hidden in people's intimacy." She recollects that their conversations sometimes touched on the theme of "strangeness in love" in the past and the present, but she does not divulge details of those conversations.

Although Adamovich never married, this book does not suggest that he had a cynical attitude toward women. But neither does the author mention any of his love affairs. About his feeling towards Odoevtseva herself the reader can judge from his words to her in Petersburg, alone in his apartment, where she and Georgi Ivanov were living temporarily: "You seem to be always... sure that you will be happy. But I am afraid that you will have to live through many difficulties... And I wish I could protect you..." At the end of this conversation, he played the piano and sang "I'd like to believe that the bright light in these eyes / Will not be darkened by life's storms..." Many years later, in Paris, in his declining years, he reminisced: "I felt towards you so much tenderness. Only tenderness..."

We know something of Adamovich's thoughts about poetry and poets, both classical and contemporary, from his *Commentaries* ("Kommentarii"). But things written for the press do not necessarily always reflect a critic's true opinion. Thus, Adamovich forecast in the *Latest News* that the artist Sharshun would have a "brilliant literary future after a hundred years". But at the same time he mockingly told an editor who wished to publish Sharshun's novel: "Don't dare print it. It'll be a sure failure."

We do not know whether Adamovich's cruel deprecation of "Balmontoviana" was fully sincere, or whether it arose from his personal resentment against Balmont. It is also possible that for the same reason he harboured some animosity towards Marina Tsvetaeva. But he did at least dedicate some verse to her: "Let us now speak at last, Marina..."

Adamovich did not consider talent a poet's most important attribute. Rather, he valued "intelligence... a feeling of measure, the ability to keep silent at the right time... pauses and that which is hidden behind the pauses. Poetry must excite and touch you."

He occasionally found Tsvetaeva as a writer uncomfortable to read because of her "egocentric mythmaking".

In her chapter about Merezhkovsky, Odoevtseva quotes another example of Adamovich's controversial critical writings. When Merezhkovsky expressed surprise at Adamovich's published praise of an obviously untalented writer, the latter replied with a sigh that it was done "Simply out of self-interest and meanness... He helped me a few times". And though Merezhkovsky excused Adamovich's motives ("There's no knowing what one might do out of meanness"), readers may be less indulgent toward such an attitude on the part of a critic whose opinions influenced the whole Russian literary world. While defending Adamovich from "praise and abuse" just as he had wished, Odoevtseva does not avoid describing his controversial traits of character. Their many years of spiritual intimacy, which, she claims, were never darkened by disputes or jealousy, gave her the right to assert that as the years went by, he became better, more responsive and more tolerant. "One has to forgive... I hate people who come to me with gossip... When repeated by somebody else, a tale becomes insulting. And it is so difficult to forgive and forget... I judge everything and everybody. Even myself, for judging..."

One of Adamovich's self-confessed weaknesses was his inability to keep a secret: "I promise solemnly and immediately blab it out... and then I am sorry." We don't know whether he regretted the damage he did to his close friends during the last war, when he spread a rumor without ever checking it's source, that Odoevtseva hosted "receptions" in her house for certain members of the German military command.

However, her chapter about him indicates that he was forgiven and that Odoevtseva retained friendly feelings toward him even after his death.

IVAN BUNIN

"Who is Irina Odoevtseva? Please, convey my regards to her and tell her that I'd like to meet her".

This was how Ivan Bunin ended a postcard that praised Odoevtseva's first short story, *The Shooting Star* ("Paduchaya zvezda"), published in the weekly newspaper *The Link* ("Zveno"), a supplement to *The Latest News* ("Poslednie Novosti") The two of them in fact met at Boris Zaitsev's jubilee in 1926 and Odoevtseva remembered the details of this meeting for the rest of her life.

Later on, she had an opportunity to hear Bunin and remember much more. They met frequently, especially at Juan les Pins, where they lived for several months in the so-called Russian House. She considered those months the most remarkable and wonderful of all her émigré years, and she described her conversations with Bunin and his everyday habits with such conviction that the reader, too, will retain a lifelong memory of him.

We see Bunin smartly dressed, slim, handsome, with his majestic looks attracting the attention of passers-by. On other occasions we see him tired, easily irritated by some trifle, wearing a coat held together by a safety pin; or at home in a camel-hair robe, slippers, and "a widebrimmed hat made of blue cotton... resembling a bird with spread wings... that had settled on his head ready for flight".

Elsewhere we meet Bunin "in a foul mood", complaining about loathsome old age and reminiscing about his impoverished youth. At another moment he charms everybody with his sharp raconteur's wit and brilliant characterizations of everyone in his story. One senses occasionally that Odoevtseva tries to suppress a sense of guilt at having to describe Bunin's unattractive character traits: admiring him as a great writer, she would also like to admire him as a human being.

Odoevtseva's reluctance may explain her assumption (which surprised even Bunin) that his haughtiness and arrogance were only a pose hiding a more modest, sensitive personality. But why would a writer hide his natural good traits under a repellent mask? The people who surround him are his readers, whose opinions he cannot but value. Indeed, we should remember that, although "not seeking people's love", he was indignant about the indifference shown to his poems and the criticism of his *Dark Alleys* ("Tyomnye allei").

Bunin once declared that "poems are fame; prose is money," and he cared deeply about his poetry. He considered *Dark Alleys* his best work, and said that the same theme would provide him enough material for another ten volumes. He was thus grievously hurt by his publisher's request to eliminate the more erotic passages from the book. He was totally convinced that he was right in his evaluation of Dostoevsky ("untalented novels"), or Chekhov ("his plays are nonsense... he did not know the life of the nobility..."), or Blok ("a stage mountebank... a circus clown..."). Bunin was just as ruthless about his contemporaries in his memoirs; he never considered that they might be concealing their better qualities, and his memoirs caused long-lasting resentment among many of his friends. Odoevtseva, too, was saddened by them, since she was convinced that Bunin was really goodhearted, noble and generous, and that only his unfortunate fate as an émigré had undermined his character. Still, a person's virtues and faults can best be judged through his interaction with others.

We learn that even in Bunin's school years he had no friends because "they were all low-cast boors". Likewise, he commented caustically about the children of his sister, who had married a railroad switchman: "they looked like common people, not at all like landowner's children, and I found it hard to believe that there was blue Bunin blood in their veins."

Evidently Bunin's arrogance was an inherent character trait even before his emigration. No one dared attribute it to poor upbringing; he always remembered his parents proudly, especially his father, whom he idealized ("an aristocrat from head to toe. Awfully frivolous. Goodhearted..."). Odoevtseva adds that Bunin never said one word of reproach to his alcoholic father, who drank away his wife's fortune and left his children in poverty. He never condemned even his father's attempt to kill his wife and would even describe the scene humorously: "mother clambering deftly up a tree like a squirrel, and father, like a hunter shooting at her." Apparently, his mother later lived much more peacefully with her daughter's family, since the only fault Bunin could find with his brother-in-law was his non-aristocratic background.

Odoevtseva wonders why Bunin, even in his successful years, never helped his adored mother and sister, only paying rare visits to the family and bringing presents for everybody.

When Bunin once compared himself to his novel's protagonist, Alyosha Arseniev, and said that as a child he had been more virtuous than his hero, Odoevtseva asked him to tell her about his best childhood deed. His story, which she masterfully recalls, could have come from Bunin's own pen. Returning from school on a fierce, frosty day, he told her, he had given away his overcoat to a beggar-boy who was blue from cold; young Bunin was later sick for a long time and almost died. When he overheard his parents say how much pain and money his sickness had cost them, he threw himself into his mother's arms, crying and promising "never to be good again".

His young listener was shocked and thought she had found the key to Bunin's heart. But he laughed mockingly and smugly, and confessed that he had invented the story. "I just told you that for fun... You listened to me so touchingly... it was almost like a scene from your Dostoevsky."

Again, the incident hardly displays Bunin's goodheartedness. And yet according to his words, in his childhood he "was just full of goodness... loved his parents... the servants and the dogs... each tree in the garden, every bird on the bough."

But Bunin as a writer knew very well what impression he made on others. He once told Odoevtseva that almost anything could make him cry -- joy, an insult, grief or jealousy. Noticing her surprise, he added ironically: "Well? Perhaps, it doesn't fit your conception of me as a fierce egotist, who thinks he is the salt of the earth?... Don't you know that I am inhumanly, devilishly proud and have always accepted honors as my due?" One can understand (though not always justify) the fact that life's vicissitudes could make a person of such character irritable and bitter. But fate was sometimes much more cruel to other Russian writers. Yet far from becoming hardened and embittered, some of them became better human beings, capable of deeper love and compassion.

Bunin's strongest love was given less to humans than to nature: "He wanted to be at one with her, to became the sky, a rock, the sea, the wind..." Generally, such love ennobles a person, but in Bunin it only deepened his resentment of writers who did not share his love ("...talentless, good for nothing, deaf,

blind moles"). He considered that even he himself wrote too little about nature -- not, as some critics said, too much -- and that the reason Dostoevsky did not write about nature was his lack of talent.
Bunin did not believe in the sincerity of diaries and letters. Readers can therefore not confidently judge his character by his letters. He evidently gave different versions of himself to different correspondents.
Odoevtseva does not try to convince us that her picture of Bunin is true-to-life. Still, she had more contact with him than most. Meeting him daily over several months, often alone, she had listened to his discourses on all sorts of themes -- on childhood, death, love, modesty, vainglory, on contemporary writers and the classics, on Anna Karenina (the most "enchanting" female character), on Natasha Rostova ("her passion to bear children... evokes only disgust"), on beauty -- on everything in fact that constitute life. He loved beauty keenly. To him it was "not only his sister, but sister and mother, and lover, and wife -- eternal femininity."

BORIS ZAITSEV

Sketching the literary portrait of Boris Konstantinovich Zaitsev, Odoevtseva did not have to choose bright hues -- apparently, they naturally emerged on the page illuminated by his modesty, goodness, hearty warmth and joy in life.
She considers his life an unusually happy one despite his experience of wars, revolutions, and years of émigré deprivation. "Happiness", she concludes, "was mainly within himself... anyone else in his place... would have lost it on the many painful stages of life's road and would have arrived at the end exhausted, embittered and unhappy, forgiving no one, not believing in anything nor hoping for anything".
Though Odoevtseva did not spell out the comparison, she must have been thinking of Bunin's comment: "What an ugly, loathsome old age I am experiencing." But celebrating his

ninetieth birthday, Zaitsev reminded Odoevtseva of her own earlier verses:

> You see, old age -- the bright evening of life --
> brings with it Aladdin's lamp...
> dissipating the tedium of the humdrum routine,
> turning everything into festivity.

Then, slowly repeating the first line, Zaitsev added: "...but very few people realize that old age is good... even very good". One must remember that at this time his beloved wife was half-paralyzed, and had for eight years been dying painfully before his eyes. Zaitsev himself had an easy death. It seemed as though life, rewarding him for his love and gratitude, yielded to death without any painful struggle.

Odoevtseva met Zaitsev rather rarely. But the pages dedicated to him make the reader see, through her eyes, a landscape by the artist Nesterov: "delicate, touching, graceful birches; the translucently radiant blueness of the Northern sky; patches of melted snow on the ground".

THE MEREZHKOVSKYS

The Green Lamp ("Zelyonaya Lampa") was the name for the literary soirées held every Sunday at the Merezhkovskys' on 11-bis rue Colonel Bonnet. These gatherings were famous not only in Paris but also in the other capitals of Europe. Yet only a select few were invited to participate.

The Green Lamp appears in the memoirs of Yuri Terapiano, Vladislav Khodasevich, V. Yanovsky and others, but Irina Odoevtseva describes everything and everybody in her own bright episodic style. She was almost always present, since her husband was the permanent chairman.

Being an observant and attentive listener, she remembers a great deal. We feel we are present at the heated debates and later at the tea-drinking, presided over by hostess Zinaida Gippius. The serving was done by Zlobin -- Merezhkovsky's secretary and "jeune fille de la maison" all in one.

Describing her first visit there by invitation, conveyed to her by Adamovich, Odoevtseva admits that she was unpleasantly shocked by Zinaida Gippius' unmannerly way of examining new guests through her lorgnette. She also disliked her looks. So, how did the hostess appear to her young guest, who didn't need a lorgnette? Odoevtseva records her "dim, swampy, colourless eyes...flat forehead. Quite a large nose. Thin, often twisting lips. Carrot-red hair... old-fashioned hairdo... the dress so motley that it hurt the eyes... on her chest a large bright-green rose, and a coral ribbon around her neck..."

Zinaida Gippius also had a lazy manner of speaking, and a desire to be liked. Yet Georgi Ivanov, who did not take to people easily, was won over the first evening. Odoevtseva confesses that her first judgment was mistaken and unfair, because at that time she could not fathom Gippius' inner life.

On the other hand, we not only "see" Merezhkovsky -- stooped, with the beard of an intellectual, and "strikingly young, lively, lynx-like, sharp-sighted eyes." But we also hear his inspired speeches, often interrupted by his wife's capricious: "No, Dimitri, I don't agree..."

They lived together until Merezhkovsky's death, never parting even for one day, always in love, though sometimes at odds: at the meetings "a fearful verbal duel would take place... both opponents would cross swords and aim clever blows at each other." But after the intellectual duel, Merezhkovsky was again the loving and attentive husband. Everybody knew that their disagreement in ideas did not disrupt the harmony of their family life. Odoevtseva calls their marriage "delightful". They never bored one another; during their walks they spoke of literature, of politics... Her logic complemented his intuition. They were, in their own way, an ideal couple.

Both of them scorned chat about the weather, health and, of course, gossip of all sorts, considering it petit-bourgeois. So they gathered around themselves people who believed in debates and discussions aimed at getting to the truth. Sundays at the Merezhkovskys' thus served as incubators of ideas. Their passionate desire to save the émigrés (if not the whole world) "from pride and self-abasement, from despair and loss of faith in the future..." recalled Vsevolzhsky's secret circle in Pushkin's time and led them to form the *Green Lamp* society. The first meeting, opened by Khodasevich, took place in February of 1927.

Mostly skimpy on details, Odoevtseva still allows the reader to witness heated arguments and debates leading to the birth of sometimes paradoxical thoughts such as Dovid Knut's suggestion that "the literary capital of Russia is now not Moscow but Paris".

Although Merezhkovsky with his enthusiasm and passionate speech always inspired the people present, they were not afraid to disagree with him. People would object, argue and heatedly defend their views. Sometimes the atmosphere became very tense. Protests could turn into shouting and foot-stamping or else into an outburst of applause.

This exchange of ideas was especially valuable to young poets and writers. Learning to think independently and freely, they also craved for an opportunity to express their thoughts and developed the art of parrying their own opponents' thrusts or accepting fair criticism. Georgi Adamovich, the best orator of the Russian émigré circles, learned enormously from these discussions, especially those with Merezhkovsky.

Odoevtseva also touches on the period when the *Green Lamp* was fading and Khodasevich and others left. But she points out that the lamp kept burning, though with reduced flame right up to the beginning of the war, and that it left a radiant memory.

Odoevtseva admits that she regularly visited those meetings not so much because of the ideas discussed there, as out of interest in the personalities of Gippius and Merezhkovsky. They always startled her by the contrast in their characters. He appeared "a more spiritual than physical being. His soul... shone in his eyes and was visible through its envelope of flesh".

Gippius' most impressive trait was her critical mind and her total inability to be carried away, express enthusiasm or admire someone else's thoughts. This self-containment probably prompted her ruthless attacks on contemporary prose and poetry back in Petersburg, where she wrote pitiless critical articles ("...idiot... prematurely born... mediocrity...") under the pseudonym Anton Kraynii. In this respect, Merezhkovsky was the direct opposite of his wife. He was easily carried away, often exaggerated people's intelligence and knowledge, and discovered depth and wisdom in thoughts that appeared commonplace to others. Thus, to Odoevtseva's surprise, he discovered special qualities in her poem *Across a White Field* ("Belym polem") which she had read in a poetry evening at the *Green Lamp*. It is worth recalling that Andrei Bely too was struck by the mysticism of her first ballad, a fact which justifies Merezhkovsky's judgment, despite the poetess' own surprise.

On that evening Gippius joked with Odoevtseva about how Merezhkovsky "fulminated" in his early poems, such as *Sakia Muni* and *The Jester's Song* ("Pesn' shuta"). She quoted his lines with deliberate pathos, and added without finishing: "But, if you could understand what power...".

We can see that the critic in Gippius could silence the loyal, loving wife (one cannot imagine Bunin's wife Vera Nikolaevna ridiculing her husband's poems). However, on one thing Gippius agreed with Merezhkovsky: he deserved the Nobel Prize. While openly declaring his hope, he could be unusually harsh towards those he perceived as rivals for the prize. Thus, he called Bunin's *Life of Arseniev* ("Zhizn' Arsenieva") a "prolonged description of the youth of a half-educated nobleman". And of his *The Village* ("Derevnya") he said: "I couldn't get into it... I keep it on my night-table in case of insomnia..."

But Bunin was equally merciless on the subject of Merezhkovsky's works. Reading about this verbal war between the two writers, one is inclined to quote Pushkin's Tatiana: "How can you with your kind heart and your intelligence be a slave to such petty feelings?"

Although Merezhkovsky was sure of his superiority, he offered to share the prize with Bunin. Bunin replied: "...I declare in advance: I don't intend to share... I believe in my own star".

Odoevtseva recollects that Merezhkovsky once called biographies "heavy rocks falling on the writer's or poet's tomb" and categorically forbade anyone to write about him after his death. ("Don't dare quote my letters... Don't nail me into my casket!"). In breaking this ban, Odoevtseva hopes to clear him of slander, asserting that "he remained a fierce enemy of Hitler, hating and despising him as before". But we also discover his view that actions do not always have to correspond with high ideals.

These memoirs reveal certain clear traits of Merezhkovsky's character. Each reader can reach an individual judgment of the man.

The Second World War brought so much confusion to concepts of morality, patriotism, heroism, and betrayal, that not all readers will feel the same way about Merezhkovsky's position. Yet since both Zinaida Gippius and Dimitri Merezhkovsky considered themselves to be unique personalities, the approval or condemnation of later generations would have been unlikely to concern them.

GEORGI IVANOV

In this volume, Odoevtseva speaks more about Georgi Ivanov than in *On the Banks of the Neva*, but less than she does about Adamovich and much less than about Bunin. She explains that writing in more detail about her husband would mean writing about herself and their life together, and this is precisely what she "was trying to avoid".

Though they lived together for thirty-seven years, their marriage, according to her, had little to do with the usual concepts of conjugal life. She quotes Adamovich's lines:

> They were illumed by a floating mysterious light
> Born by a flickering flame for which there is no name.

To help the reader understand Georgi Ivanov, she returns to his childhood, to his family who knew luxury as well as ruin, poverty, and the bitterness of loss. One reads these pages of his biography like an engrossing novella. The loss of his dearly loved father made "Yurochka" lose his faith in God, because his childhood prayers were not heard. We learn about Ivanov's infatuations: first painting, then chemistry, and lastly poetry, which he considered his life's work. Awaiting impatiently the day when he could discard his cadet's uniform, he wrote poetry, was successfully published and was recommended to Gumilyov as "a future Pushkin".

Yet only after he had outgrown his infatuation with "Egofuturism" and had published a collection of poetry called *Embarkation for Cythera* ("Otplytie na ostrov Tsitera") did he become acquainted with Gumilyov and Akhmatova and was accepted into the Poets' Guild. Only then did he feel that he was an adult and a real poet. But Odoevtseva believes that many poets, especially Russian ones, continue to suffer from infantilism, and that Georgi Ivanov was never cured of it.

During the First World War Ivanov successfully wrote poems for the journal *The Creek* ("Lukomorye"). He was lucky in all his undertakings. Despite the fact that his premature marriage to a French girl was rather short-lived, his easily obtained divorce (his wife left with their child for France) soon consoled him. His marriage to Odoevtseva afforded him the opportunity to write while living comfortably abroad. Odoevtseva's father, who lived in Riga, provided them with a steady income until his death in 1932, and then -- with a large inheritance.

Thus his lot in life emerged as rather satisfactory and the sobriquet of "poète maudit" was absolutely groundless. It was only in 1948, when Odoevtseva lost all her sources of income, that their ordeals began. Even then, the weight fell principally on Odoevtseva's shoulders, since Georgi Ivanov was entirely incapable of earning money.

"He would write only when he felt like it... he considered the work of a journalist harmful to a poet... and wrote prose with difficulty." Only on his *Decay of the Atom* ("Raspad Atoma") did he work with enthusiasm. In contrast to Gumilyov, who never spent a day without writing a line, Georgi Ivanov wrote only when he was inspired. He never rose before noon, he loved to read detective stories (not less than one a day) and stuck to these habits even when life was very difficult for them and they existed mainly on royalties from Odoevtseva's stories and novels.

Negotiating with publishers, theatres, and cinema companies about his wife's film scripts, he gradually became a sort of impresario for her.

Yet Ivanov was called the best poet in the emigration. In the United States it was said that he would be nominated for the Nobel Prize "if the political situation permitted it".

He accepted his popularity very ironically. Thus, when an over-enthusiastic critic once brought him an article headed "Georgi Ivanov -- the greatest poet of the world", he remarked, straightfaced: " 'Yes, that's correct but you have to add 'the world and its environs'. "

Though he had never studied the art of writing poetry, he wrote so easily that his poems seemed to "fall complete from heaven." Odoevtseva describes her excitement and the impression of a miracle when one morning, at breakfast, he recited to her a poem that had come to him there and then:

> Mist all around, just mist... The desert listens
> To God. Tomorrow's still so far away.
> There Lermontov walks on the road, and silence
> Reverberates the ringing of his spurs.

But Ivanov's poems did not always arouse her admiration. Thus, in the last period of his life, playing the role of *poète maudit*, Ivanov wrote: "All night I walked from bar to bar..." Odoevtseva objected, as Gumilyov had to Akhmatova: "What are you doing? One is liable to believe it..."

In describing his past, she tries to help us understand him. But despite their thirty-seven years of life together, she herself confesses that he often appeared to her "strange... mysterious'', and she could not always understand him because of his complex, many-sided personality. Yet she assures us that of all the remarkable people she met in life he was ''the most remarkable''. She quotes Gippius who considered him ''the ideal poet, a poet of pure chemical substance'', and adds that he was ''the absolute incarnation of a poet''. Ivanov's treatment of his wife can be deduced from his frequent request: ''Please, call if you will be late, I'll be worried...''

In Odoevtseva's chapter on Bunin we find his opinion of Georgi Ivanov's attitude towards his wife. During a rather prolonged walk with Odoevtseva, when she kept repeating, ''Georgi will be worried'', he accused her of being controlled by her husband. ''Of course, he'll worry... he loves you, loves you too much. But there is no use in this love. Only anxiety and suffering. I know... from experience.'' We shall never know whether or not she agreed with Bunin about such ''great love''.

But when Odoevtseva grew ill from overwork (poverty forced her to write as much as fifteen hours a day) and the doctors suspected she had tuberculosis, her first thought was for her husband: ''For God's sake, don't tell Georgi, tell him that it is simply bronchitis...'' And she began preparing herself for death. Fortunately, the doctors were wrong, and she got well. But the fear of losing her and his attempts to help her during her illness undermined Ivanov's own health.

He was admitted to an old people's home in Hyeres, of southern France. But the climate was not good for his heart, and in 1958 he died. They had earlier been refused admission to Gagny (near Paris), where in September of the same year the poet's widow went alone. In a poem dated August 1958, Ivanov wrote:

> I am dying, although I could still live on
> About ten years or maybe even twenty.
> Yet no one feels compassion, no one helps.
> Say, how can I not laugh about it?

Odoevtseva explains the regrettable indifference (if not animosity) which surrounded her and her husband during the war years, and her reaction to unfounded rumors that they were collaborating with the Nazis. Strangely, it was their best friend Adamovich who had spread slanderous gossip already mentioned in the chapter about him, "embellishing it with the flowers of his fantasy". One can only ascribe her continued friendship with him until his death to Odoevtseva's innate goodness.

YURI TERAPIANO

"It will be a sin if you don't write your memoirs about Petersburg. Nobody but you can do it," Yuri Terapiano persistently urged Odoevtseva in Gagny, where she lived after Georgi Ivanov's death.

She had seen this tall, dark-haired man at the Green Lamp, but then he had not been one of her close friends. Yet Terapiano was to play an important role in her life. She credited him with giving her the strength to withstand human malice and return to literature, and not give in to the bouts of pessimism that were so foreign to her nature. Their friendship, which lasted over twenty years, was never clouded by disagreement or misunderstanding.

It seems that neither Gumilyov nor even Georgi Ivanov recognized her talent to the extent that Terapiano did, and she recalls this with deep gratitude. He was the first president of the "Union of Young Poets", which he formed in Petersburg in 1920. His second volume of verses, *Insomnia*, sold out completely. But when he became the literary critic for *Russkaya mysl'*, in Paris, readers lost interest in his poetry, a fact which grieved him sorely.

Odoevtseva does not describe Terapiano's creative work. Nor does she speak much about his illness and death. It is as a loving personality that he appears on the few pages of a chapter devoted to him. She recalls him in the evenings in Meudon ("Medonskie vechera") at René Guerra's, their long walks, or hours spent in a café where he shared with her his thoughts about his next article and, of course, about the past.

As a child Terapiano wanted to become a traffic policeman, but later thought he might become an archaeologist. He then took a great interest in ancient history, classical poetry, and in translating ancient poems. At sixteen he inherited a substantial fortune from his uncle, an archaeologist, who had hoped that his nephew would follow in his footsteps.

Knowing that Terapiano's biography and collected articles (prepared by the poetess Aglaida Shimansky) were to be published in Paris by René Guerra, Odoevtseva describes only a few episodes of their life in Gagny. She concludes: "Though years have passed since his death, I know that no one ever has or ever will take his place in my life."

YAKOV GORBOV

Yakov Nikolayevich Gorbov, Odoevtseva's husband from 1978 till his death in September 1982, is mentioned in her memoirs very briefly, and mainly as a writer.

At the conclusion of the book she provides a short biography, then describes his infatuation with her novel *Isolde*. Not only did he read the novel many times in Paris; he even carried it with him to the front in 1941 and brought it home again despite being wounded. All this he told her at their first meeting after the war.

Gorbov was a writer in his own right, but his literary career had been interrupted by years spent at the bedside of his first wife, during her mental illness.

Remembering what Terapiano had done for her, Odoevtseva decided to do the same for Yakov Gorbov - to bring him back to life and literature. He was well known in France as the author of novels in French, a language he had mastered in his childhood in Moscow, where he was born to a well-to-do family. One of his novels, *Les Condamnés*, had been awarded the "Four Judges" prize. Odoevtseva translated his novel *Madame Sophie* into Russian.

After the death of Gorbov's wife, he and Odoevtseva married. She writes that his love had always deeply touched her, yet because of his heart operation and serious illness her hope to bring him back into Russian literature was never realized. Their marriage lasted less than four years. Odoevtseva concludes the chapter about him with the hope that all of his French novels would be translated into Russian someday and made available to readers in the West and in Russia.

YURI ANNENKOV

Odoevtseva's acquaintances were not limited to authors. Her interest in art often helped her meet artists. This is not surprising, since her literary portraits have the quality of paintings.

We meet one of those artists, Yuri Annenkov, who was famous in pre-revolutionary Russia for his portraits of Sologub, Akhmatova, Zamyatin, and others. The Petropolis publishing company in Petersburg had commissioned Annenkov to paint a portrait of Odoevtseva. Later they met in Paris, and she devotes to him several pages filled with humor and sadness. A nostalgic flashback to days in Petersburg alternates with comical episodes of a visit to Paris by the Soviet writers Erenburg and Simonov.

She also recalls Gumilyov's words about Annenkov: "He is quicksilver, not a man... God gave him a devilish, hurricane-like energy... He finds time for everything, even for writing poems." Indeed Annenkov always remained a "human hurricane", succeeding as a portrait painter, decorator, critic, and also as writer and author of *A Tale About Trifles* and *Diary of My Encounters -- Cycle of Tragedies* ("Povest' o pustyakakh"; "Dnevnik moikh vstrech -- Tsikl tragedii").

Odoevtseva describes a nature trait of Annenkov unknown to his many friends -- the self-control that allowed him to conceal his heart's and soul's distress. For instance, on the day his adored wife, the young actress Natalie Belyaev, left him, he went with his daughter to a reception for some Soviet visitors. On the way there, he laconically told Odoevtseva what had happened and immediately begged her not to console or pity him. During the reception he was the same Annenkov, lively and full of fun. Even on the way home he remained in control; only at the hotel door did he suddenly break down: "Don't go... I'm afraid to be alone..." He again stunned her by masking his despair behind an affected calmness when she promised to stay with him for a while. While they walked round and round the block, he chatted about neutral things: the reception, poetry reading, old days in Petersburg, etc. Then, just as suddenly, he stopped at her hotel and said goodnight, adding: "Thank you. I'll always remember..."

Perhaps he did remember, but he never mentioned the explosion of despair, witnessed by Odoevtseva, when out of compassion for his grief she walked with him through the streets of Paris until she was exhausted.

SERGEI SHARSHUN

Odoevtseva's recollections about another artist, Sergei Sharshun, are written in a different key. He represented the avant-garde, and in Picasso's opinion was "one of the best". He lived in Paris before the First World War. Odoevtseva describes his first visit in Paris to the Green Lamp circle, where he was greatly respected as an artist. Yet none of the group believed in his genius as a poet and writer.

Odoevtseva met him again in 1973, forty years after their first encounter. He had hardly changed, and at the age of eighty-seven still talked excitedly about his many travels, which opened for him "a new world of colours and light... a new outlook on art".

A reader who has never seen any of Sharshun's paintings can share Odoevtseva's delight at the artist's *White Symphonies* ("Belye simfonii") and at his studio. She makes us see birches... not French ones "crooked and painfully bent... these have a real Russian bearing." We share Odoevtseva's admiration for the magical realism of the artist's flamingos, penguins and walruses. We feel all that is behind and around the painting, "the vibrating... almost radiant air". It is not surprising that

Sharshun says he reread Odoevtseva's article about him and his art in *Russkaya mysl* ' no less than twenty-seven times. The same vividness of description makes us remember the strange gesticulations of Sharshun and his hands with their oddly extended thumbs'', Poplavsky's ''seemingly blind'' eyes, Bunin's proud bearing, and many other poignant details.

With amazing word combinations that serve her as an artist's palette, she creates portraits of her heroes and, by breathing new life into them, helps us who are alive to see them, hear their voices, and share with them the scale of their emotions, from dark despair to radiant joy. It seems certain that in the genre of memoir literature Odoevtseva's writings will always occupy a special place.

* * *

Bibliography

In Russian: *Dvor Chudes*. Stikhi (pg., 1992); *Angel Smerti* (Paris, 1927; 2nd ed. 1938); *Izol'da* (Berlin, 1931); *Zerkalo* (Brussels, 1939); *Kontrapunkt* (Paris, 1951); *Stikhi napisanbnye vo vremia bolezni* (Paris, 1952); *Ostav' nadezhdu navsegda* (NY, 1954); *"God Zhizni,"* Vozrozhdenie 63-68 (1958); *Desyat' let*. Stikhi (Paris, 1961); *Odinochestvo* (Washington, DC, 1965); *Na beregakh Nevy*. Vospominaniia (Washington DC, 1967; 2nd ed. M., 1988); *Zlataia tsep'* (Paris 1975); *Portret v rifmovannoi rame* (Paris, 1976); *"Na beregakh Seny,"* RMysl' 1978-81, and (Paris, 1983); 2nd ed. M., 1989); "Ia slovno by i ne uezzhala iz Rossii" [Interview], RM*ysl'* (Mar. 3, 1983): 8; poems in *Muza Diaspory* (Frankfurt/M., 1960), *Ogoniok* 1989 11, and *Slovo* 1989 9.

In Translation: *Out of Childhood*, D. Nachesen, tr. (NY, 1930); *Ljuka der Backfish*, W.E. Groeger, tr. (1930); *Laisse toute esperance* (Paris, 1948); *All Hope Abandon*, F. Reed, tr. (NY, 1949); *"Abandona toda esperanza,"* Luis de Caralt, tr. (Barcelona, 1949); poetry in *"Days with Bunin,"* K. Gavrilovich, tr. *RR* 1971: 111-23, 226-39, Markov and Sparks, and *A Russian Cultural Revival*, Temira Pachmuss, tr. (Knoxville TN, 1981).

References: Abyzov; Bristol; Exhov and Shamurin; Foster; Gusman; Kasak; Matsuev KhL 1971-25; Sztein; Tarasenkov; Terras; Vitman; Vladislavlev *LDV*; Wilson // *"Tri reki vremeni,"* LitGaz 1987 12:5; A. Ar've, *"Dvazhdy dva -- piat's pliusom*. Stikhi Iriniy Odoevtsevoi," Zvezda 1987 9: 78-79; Nina Berverova, *The Italics Are Mine*, Philippe REadley, tr. (NY, 1969): 552; Ella Bobrova, *"Irina odoevtseva,"* NZh 146 (1982); Aleksandr Gidoni, *"Skvoz" zven'ia tsepi zolotoi,"* Sovr 1975 7: 62; Andrei Sedykh, *"Poèziia Iriny odoevtsevoi,"* NRS (June 13, 1975); Gleb Struve, *"Pis'ma o russkoi poèzii,"* RMysl' 1923 1-2; V.S. Yanovsly, *Elysian Fields*, Isabella and V.S. Yanaovsky trs. (DeKalb IL, 1987).

List of Anthologies with Irina Odoevtseva's Poems

Peterburg v stikhotvoreniyakh russkikh poetov (Editor and Introduction: G. Alekseev. - 114p.)

Yakor: Anthology of Émigré Poetry. (Editors: G.V. Adamovich and M.L. Kantor. "Petropolis", 1936 -242p.)

Krug: Almanac. - "Parabola", 1938, 187p.

Russky sbornik: Vol I - Paris, "Podorozhnik", 1946, 203p

Orion: Literary Almanac (Editors: Yu. Odarchenko, V. Smoliansky and A. Shaikevich.Paris, 1947, 162p.)

Na zapade: anthology of Russian Émigré Poetry (Editor and Introduction: Yu. Ivanov - New York, Chekhov Publishing, 1953, 398p.)

Sodruzhestvo: Contemporary Russian Émigré Poetry (Editor and Introduction: T. Fesenko - Washington, Victor Kamkin Publishing, 1966, 559p.)

Muza Diaspory: Selected Poems of Émigré Poets 1920-1960. Editor : Y.K. Terapiano, Frankfurt/M. "Posev", 1960, 360 p.